The Gifts of
Grace & Gratitude

*Inspirational Stories of Women Who Transformed
Their Lives by Living in the Space of
Appreciation, Trust, and Faith*

Powerful You!
PUBLISHING
Sharing Wisdom ~ Shining Light

THE GIFTS OF GRACE & GRATITUDE

Inspirational Stories of Women Who Transformed Their Lives by Living in the Space of Appreciation, Trust, and Faith

Copyright © 2016

Published by: Powerful You! Inc. USA
powerfulyoupublishing.com

Library of Congress Control Number: 2016954142

Sue Urda and Kathy Fyler –First Edition

ISBN: 978-0-9970661-3-5

First Edition November 2016

Self Help / Women's Studies

Printed in the United States of America

Dedication

*This book is dedicated to all seekers
who open themselves to
the magic and mystery of life.*

Table of Contents

May You Be
Guided by Grace...

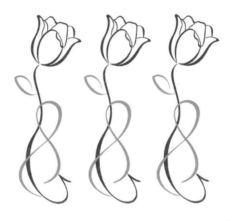

And Filled with
Gratitude!

Foreword

When asked by Sue Urda if I would write a foreword to The Gifts of Grace and Gratitude, I was elated. Not only because these two virtues are very close to my heart and life's work, but also because of the instant connection I felt when speaking to Sue on the phone about the project. My internal compass of gratitude always points me in the direction where love, connection, and peace reside. That was my experience of Sue and this book—peace.

I believe when we make a decision to share our hearts and experiences with the world miracles occurs. When I learned that this book was just that, a collection of amazing authors sharing their heartfelt stories, I was honored to be in service to it.

My path to gratitude has been nothing short of a journey of awakening. I believe Grace and Gratitude generate the same thing: A deep sense of being-ness in the present moment. Grace is the trust we feel when we realize that everything is exactly as it should be and we are grateful for it. It happens in that brief space generated when we have that knowingness that we are all whole, perfect, and complete. Grace is the miracle; Gratitude brings you there.

My first awakened encounter with Grace and Gratitude was in the form of an eighty-year old man that would forever alter my life and the lives of so many others. I was at an airport in New York, and I was rushing toward the gate to catch my flight. I accidentally ran into this man, and we both nearly fell to the ground. I immediately started bracing myself, as I was certain this man would give me a lecture and tell me what a horrible person I was. But I was wrong. Instead, the man, whose name was Don Warms, turned to me and hugged me and said, "No worries, I bet you do this all the time!" Then he laughed and turned to me with a grandfatherly look just before he took his granddaughter by the hand and walked away. I was standing there watching him leave, and I suddenly felt an intense feeling of gratitude for life and people. Don had simply showed me that life didn't have to be the way I thought it was. He was an interruption to the story or belief I had been subscribing to my whole life. This interruption was a miracle. It was Grace.

I wanted to give him something in return, a token of my appreciation. I realized how important it is that we act from love and that we honor and appreciate each other—no matter what.

I boarded the plane, still in awe over the "moment of gratitude" that just occurred. I was reflecting on my whole life as I sat in my seat looking out over the beautiful clouds beneath me, and I realized, "I am flying." Something awakened in me. I felt a sense of calm and a sense of deep gratitude. I wanted to share this with the world. A vision and a deeper sense of purpose were emerging. I started thinking, *What if we had something we could give each other in that moment of appreciation and gratitude, a token of appreciation? A coin! I got it! I was going to create a coin—a token that simply says, "Thank you for making a difference in my day."* I also decided I would put a unique serial number on each coin so it could be tracked online as it travels from person to person. I was going to make a difference in the world!

It turned out Don Warms was on my flight, and I had a chance to thank him again, get his contact information, and tell him what I was committed to create because of him. That day, TOFA (Token of Appreciation) was born.

A year later, to the date, I had 1,000 tokens manufactured and numbered, and I launched the tracking website. That day, I drove to Don Warms' house unannounced to give him token No. 1 and thank him for making a difference in my LIFE. On this day, I started something I call "The Giving Year." I made a commitment to give away one token every day for 365 days and document every "Token Moment" on YouTube. I had no idea what this one-year journey would do for me and for the people I encountered. In fact, some days were difficult days, where I was simply in my "stuff" and was not "feeling it." These days I learned some of the most valuable lessons. I was choosing from committed action and vision rather than choosing from how I was feeling. Once I went out in the world, *generating* a moment to be grateful for, I realized how important it is for us to stand in gratitude, appreciation, and committed action to create amazing results in our lives.

Toward the end of the Giving Year, I started seeing amazing

changes in my personal life, both financially and emotionally. I manifested the house I wanted to live in. I say "manifest" because I was becoming more and more aware of what I was creating, and I realized it was not chance that threw all these amazing opportunities my way. I was opening a space for it by standing in gratitude and appreciation. I created the relationships I wanted. Money was beginning to flow. And most importantly, joy and peace were now a way of life, a state of mind, rather than something outside of me to strive for.

I believe these moments of grace and gratitude are around us all the time. The question is if we are awake enough to notice them. Once we are able to find that space, that small moment of presence, in the midst of our hectic lives, we will begin to experience the small miracles that constitute our life. Because that is what life is, an abundance of miracles happening in every moment.

When I teach about gratitude, I talk about 3 versions of gratitude. They all bring peace and love to any moment, yet they are each concerned with a different time; the past, present, or the future. When we are in Comparative Gratitude we are looking at something that has already occurred in the past (even if it was 5 minutes ago). We may say, "I am grateful because I am better off than someone else" or "I am grateful that I am not in that relationship any more" etc. You are comparing where you are to either someone or something else, or to where you have been.

Declarative Gratitude is concerned with the future. This is when you bring the future into the present as you declare what you want (because you don't have it). For instance, "I am grateful now that I have the house I always wanted", even though you do not have it yet. This is a powerful way, similar to affirmations, to bring your future visions and goals into existence sooner.

A State of Gratitude, the third version, happens only in the present moment. It is a state, similar to joy, in which we have an understanding (or a deep connection) that everything is as it should be, and we are grateful that it is. Gratitude is the highest level of consciousness in taking full responsibility as the creator of our reality. When we can accept everything as being exactly as it should be and at the same time stand in gratitude for it, we begin to manifest peace and love.

Gratitude is a virtue I hold near to my heart. When I stand in a place of gratitude, my life is richer. Gratitude is the highest state of consciousness. Gratitude brings us to the present moment, it brings us to Grace. It is the foundation of all abundance.

In Gratitude,
Jo Englesson
Creative Peacemaker

Introduction

You are undoubtedly a seeker, a truth finder, and an individual with a purpose. You know in the depths of your being that you are surrounded by grace, even when you do not feel it. You know that there is much to be grateful for, even if you can't put your finger on it. And you know you are blessed, even though life doesn't always go your way.

And although you know these things innately, you have a deep desire to feel them. You wish to be more fully enveloped in the beauty of the gifts of grace and gratitude with each breath you take, with each moment you live.

The authors in this book feel your longing for grace; they have longed for it too. Somewhere within their life journeys they discovered the real truth of grace. They learned that grace is an inside job and it comes to us from external forces too.

The inside job is you consciously opening and allowing for the bounty of life to unfold before you and within you. It is you realizing that the choices you make either cut you off or open you up to goodness that is present in every person and situation you encounter. And the inside job is personal to you—it can't be measured or achieved without your consent, your awareness, and your own discernment that it is truly grace that you are witnessing, receiving, and living.

As you read these stories you will see that grace was found in the deeds and words of individuals willing to comfort and care for these women. Grace was bestowed in the form of a friend, an unexpected kindness, or even as a disease, a burning down and rising up from the ashes, or the loss of a loved one. You will bear witness to the individual "aha's" and the illumination of pure grace in the soul of the writers.

Yes, grace has many faces, each of them as common as the next in their feeling place, and yet each unique in their expression. In these tales you will read not only about grace, but also the overwhelming gratitude for the lessons learned, the blessings given, and the new paths taken.

There's no mistake that grace is a gift—a gift that is given to each of us. You don't have to do anything to earn grace, instead it is something that is bestowed upon you as a birthright. The truth is that grace is available to you in each moment, and your only responsibility is to allow it in, to feel it's presence.

Having been touched by grace, these authors know the magic it holds, bringing with it a sense of aliveness and peace at the same time. And although you may not have called it that you, too, have been touched by grace.

Our wish is that you be open to feel the immensity of grace in your own life. As you feel it, name it and affirm it; for once you affirm grace its' beauty is multiplied and you will feel truly grateful.

Go in grace, live in gratitude.

with much love for you,
Sue Urda
Powerful You! Inc.

Affirmations

I am blessed with beauty and grace in each moment.

I am filled with gratitude.

I am surrounded by opportunity and love.

I live in the abundance of life.

Life is here FOR me.

I am a loved and loving child of God.

I am healthy, and vibrant, and strong.

I am purposeful and passionate as I move through my day.

I use my gifts to serve all who need me.

I am a divine expression of grace in action.

I am open to receive great good.

I am at peace.

Healing into Life
Wanda Buckner

Twelve years ago, life as I knew it collapsed. My beloved partner died. Not because he was ill. Not because he was elderly. Not because he had a progressive debilitating disease or was in a coma. He died due to a cascade of events following a medical error that misdiagnosed BOOP—Bronchial Obliterans Obstructive Pneumonia—as lung cancer.

Lloyd's right lung resection went well; however, during the night the lung collapsed. Complications followed and another surgery. I thought if I loved enough and believed enough, he would live. And he did; but it was a miserable life. A tracheostomy tube carried oxygen-rich air from a ventilator directly to his lungs. A feeding tube directly in his stomach provided nourishment. A catheter collected urine. These measures were meant to be temporary. However, his lung was unable to recover; the ventilator and all that went with it became permanent.

Lloyd could not eat. He could not talk. He could not go outside. He could not come home. The next move would be from the hospital critical care unit to a skilled nursing facility capable of handling ventilator patients. We would live from one medical crisis to another until his body gave out. Lloyd requested life support be ended. He wrote, "I've had a good life. I have no regrets."

Five-and-a-half months after what was expected to be a non-remarkable surgery followed by a six-week recovery, I authorized withdrawal of all treatment. I held Lloyd's hand while the morphine was increased and the ventilator oxygen decreased. Even though his chest raised and lowered with the artificial breath of the ventilator, I knew he was gone. So was the future we'd planned together.

I was numb after months of living between his bedside and our RV parked in the hospital lot responding to crisis after crisis. My life partner dying was difficult enough, but that it was the unnecessary result of a medical error made it even harder. Thankfully, my friends and grief support group gently held me in the days and months that followed.

The grief group gave me perspective—I was not the most wronged spouse in the world. A widower shared pictures of his beautiful wife with a quarter of her face carved away in an unsuccessful attempt to stop the cancer. A young man came with his newborn baby; his wife had died in childbirth. A woman's brother had died in jail. Spouses mourned the long, slow death of Alzheimer's and death from debilitating, progressive diseases that took their loved ones one breath at a time.

Ironically, I discovered I had much to be grateful for. In the hospital, staff had assisted Lloyd to sit upright so we could follow a seated exercise program on TV. We sorted through boxes of unmarked photos and organized them into memory albums. We spent days together that under other circumstances would have been filled with work. Lloyd's mind remained clear. Only relatives could visit, so his friends remembered him as the vital man he was when he entered the hospital.

Despite the circumstances that led to Lloyd choosing death, I struggled to move in ways that would tip my universe toward peace and away from grief; toward hope rather than despair. I tried to maintain our life as it had been. I took the grandkids camping, but Lloyd had been the one who baited the hooks and killed and gutted the flopping, gasping fish they caught. Lloyd was the gentle force behind the flowers and birds that filled our yard. He had a gift for gardening; I did not. I continued to bowl on our mixed doubles team, but without Lloyd the joy was gone. I returned to grant writing, but my zest for the competitive process had dulled. I had no vision of my future, much less a plan for the day. I was sure the best times of my life were over.

The cancer rate was high in my grief group, perhaps due to years of caretaking, perhaps due to many of us not caring if we lived or died. When Marla developed a suspicious spot on her lung, she declared it a gift. She took to her bed, stopped her Parkinson's and heart medications, and died within the month. I was angry that she didn't choose life; instead she chose to join her deceased husband. For her, death was not the enemy.

I was determined to live. I knew Lloyd didn't mean for us both to die. But how to live? The love of my life was gone forever. I had no interest in work or anything else. The past sucked me backward into grief and despair. I tried to find meaning in Lloyd's untimely death and in my drastically altered life.

Vaughn, also a member of my grief group, was diagnosed with terminal cancer and given three months to live. At the same time, his younger sister, Jane, a long-term dialysis patient, decided treatment was too onerous. She was ready to quit. She invited her extended family to one last party, knowing without dialysis she would live only five to seven days. Vaughn wanted to use his sister's gathering to tell his family that he too was dying. He asked me to come with him for support.

Jane hosted a splendid reunion, full of laughter, pictures, and family memories. She skipped her dialysis appointment that afternoon and that evening refused her medications. When Vaughn and I arrived the next morning, Jane was lying on a small rug in front of the kitchen refrigerator in extreme agitation, spewing angry accusations. A hospice nurse sat at the kitchen table, her notebook open in front of her. She informed the family that hospice could not get involved because Jane was experiencing a psychotic break. She recommended they call 911. With that, she closed her notebook and left.

Vaughn and his brother picked up the corners of the rug Jane was lying on and used it to carry her to the living room couch. I sat beside her and spoke softly of a beautiful beach in an attempt to use a guided imagery method I'd heard thirty years ago. Eventually Jane calmed enough to be coaxed to her bedroom. I closed the door and continued to talk to her in a low, soothing voice. As I talked, I felt an overwhelming compulsion to hold my hands about six inches above her body and move them slowly from above her head to below her feet. I did this three or four times; I don't know why. It just seemed like the thing to do.

Jane relaxed immediately. She whispered that it was like "going to Nirvana." She fell asleep and I tiptoed out. The next day, Jane asked her family to call me. I went into her bedroom and closed the door. Jane shared bits of her life and writings with me. When she tired, she asked me to run my hands above her body like I had before. As I did this, she drifted into sleep. Seeing how my presence calmed Jane, her daughter asked me to come visit every morning and evening. I always saw Jane alone with the door closed. I didn't want anyone to see the strange motions I made.

Five days later, hospice was involved. Pain medications were ordered and would be available the next day. An aide came and bathed Jane, but it didn't go well. When I arrived, Jane's mouth was bleeding from biting her cheek. Her arms were clutched tightly against her stiff body. With death imminent, I invited Jane's family to gather around her bedside. They watched as I moved my hands over Jane's body from above her head to below her feet, slowly repeating the motion until she calmed. I slipped out to leave Jane with her family. She died peacefully an hour later. The next day, Jane's daughter sought me out to ask where she could learn to do what I had done. I had no idea; I didn't know what it was.

The trauma of Jane's death overshadowed Vaughn's news of untreatable cancer. Based on Lloyd's experience, Vaughn made an appointment at the Mayo Clinic for a second opinion. There he learned his cancer was operable.

I bought Vaughn a book on cancer treatment options. Browsing through it, I found a chapter on alternative therapies. A paragraph on Therapeutic Touch described exactly what happened with Jane. I was stunned. The text said that some people without training could do this work. I immediately bought Delores Krieger's book, *The Therapeutic Touch: How to Use Your Hands to Help or to Heal.*

I took Krieger's book with me to read while I waited my turn at Providence Hospital to have the required tuberculosis test for volunteers. On the table beside me was a brochure for a Healing Touch Level I training at that hospital, that weekend. I called the coordinator and enrolled.

I completed Level 1 and 2 in quick succession and participated in the bi-monthly Healing Touch practice sessions where we exchanged mini-treatments. The healing energy that flowed through me to Jane now flowed to others honed by the techniques I learned in class. In turn, healing energy flowed through my fellow practitioners to me. I cried on the treatment table, releasing deeply held grief from Lloyd's death. So began the long healing process that changed my life, healed my grief, and allowed me to love—and be loved—again.

I am deeply grateful that Lloyd's death was not in vain. Vaughn learned from Lloyd's experience and lived to remarry. I'm sure others also sought second opinions knowing what happened in my life. I learned death is a release. Now I know that when people say they want six more months of life, what they mean is they want six months of quality life, not six months of pain, misery, and continuing debilitation. Lloyd had the grace to release himself. In doing so, he released me.

The concept of energy work was foreign to me and my academic world of measurement and analysis. But, intrigued at the possibilities, I completed Healing Touch Levels 3 and 4. The prerequisite for Level 5, was to document one hundred healing sessions. Despite my experience with Jane, I still doubted I could do this work. I offered free Healing Touch sessions in exchange for a frank evaluation by my clients of their experiences. The results were astounding. Almost a third of the clients' issues were 75% to 100% resolved! One hundred percent said they received other benefits from the sessions in addition to those they came for. Within three months I closed my proposal writing business and opened "Healing Energy Services" for people and animals.

During those early sessions, I began to see scenes from my clients' lives. I heard deceased people speak. I was aware of spiritual beings present in the room. I enrolled in more classes, seeking understanding. In a CDM Spiritual Center class, we created an object from a lump of clay. I fashioned a lovely, multi-petalled rose. I took pride in showing my rose to the class. Then the instructor told us to destroy our creations. I didn't want to! I wanted to keep my beautiful rose as a memento. Nonetheless, I mashed my rose back into a formless lump. The point of the lesson was that destruction is just as necessary as creation. We can't keep creating and creating and creating without destruction. The world would run out of room. We would run out of room. Both processes are necessary and equally valuable.

I had created a wonderful life and career with Lloyd. I wanted it to go on forever. However, its destruction allowed a new possibility that would never have manifested had I not been drifting without purpose or direction. I am grateful that I did not immerse myself in busyness after Lloyd's death and for the space that allowed me to create a new life.

The years with Lloyd were a resting place of love and support. Now, I have a different partner and a different mission. This time is equally as wonderful as the time before. I am deeply grateful for the life I had with Lloyd and the grace that got me through the devastating loss and grief after his death. I am equally grateful for the love-filled life I have now and the opportunity be of service in ways I never imagined possible.

Lloyd healed into death. I healed into life.

ABOUT THE AUTHOR: Wanda Buckner is an author, speaker, teacher, Healing Touch Practitioner, and Reiki Master. After discovering that she had healing hands, Wanda began a journey of self-discovery. Asking, "What else is possible?" led her to energy healing, clairvoyance, mediumship, interspecies communication, and hypnotherapy. Profound results from early healing sessions prompted Wanda to close her grant-writing business and open Healing Energy Services, transforming the lives of people and animals. Her book, *Choosing Energy Therapy: A Practical Guide to Healing Options for People and Animals*, provides many answers about energy work. Wanda encourages others to also ask that key question: What else is possible? Based in Olympia, Washington, Wanda works with clients everywhere.

Wanda Buckner, EdD, HTCP, HTACP, CHt, Reiki Master
Healing Energy Services
HealingEnergyServices.com
wanda@HealingEnergyServices.com
360-491-3187

Jewels by the Sea...
A Creation Story
Linda Ronelle Jalving

Every creation has a gestation period. In the mammal world, opossums have the shortest gestation period at 12 to 13 days, and elephants the longest at 23 months. In the world of entrepreneurship, a business gestation period can be an infinitesimal moment to what might seem like an eternity. For me, it took 20 years!

Four years in a community college studying everything from music to English to river rafting left me floundering with the question "What do I want to do when I grow up?" I finally received an associate's degree in landscape design, but "circumstances" and the fact that I have always been starry-eyed for beautiful and shiny things, led me instead to a career in jewelry store management in Portland, Oregon. In 1982 I miraculously received a transfer to open stores for our company in my dream city San Diego, California.

My pal and work associate Val was visiting from Portland and I wanted to show her the dazzling charms of La Jolla, a lovely seaside village in San Diego. A quaint courtyard lured us with a tempting "Estate Jewelry" sign. We strolled up the brick steps into an enchanting shop filled with yummy jewelry—if only the little morsels could talk.

"Wouldn't it be fun to own a jewelry store like this someday?" I casually asked.

After establishing the first couple of stores in San Diego, I was ready to become further involved in the community, so I joined Soroptimists International of La Jolla—a global volunteer organization working to improve the lives of women and girls. There, I "coincidentally" met the owner of the very same charming estate jewelry store I had visited.

"Cecilia," I said, "if you're ever thinking about selling your jewelry store, please let me be the first to know!"

It would take 16 years, two more jewelry store openings with my company, and a switch to Rotary International, another service organization that had begun admitting women, before I received that life-changing call from Cecilia.

"Linda, I'm moving to Florida to retire and be closer to my sons—are you still interested in my shop?"

Although my heart skipped a beat, I told her I needed some time to consider it. I hadn't thought about it since my initial curiosity, and in the years since I had become very invested in my present job. Cecelia agreed, and from the moment I hung up the phone it was all I could think about! I called my best friend, Debbie, and others, I made a pros and cons list, I prayed and asked my church friends to pray with me.

Then I had a vivid dream. I was behind the counter in that darling little shop helping some European visitors and smiling from ear to ear. I awoke with a start, and the thought of living that dream sent my spirit soaring! I called Cecelia the next day ready to make an offer within my budget, only to hear that she had been offered more than I could afford by a couple who also bought her condo and agreed to keep her cat. It seemed to be the best for all concerned except for me. My heart shed a tear. The thought of leaving a steady paycheck, four weeks of paid vacation, full benefits, and a profit-sharing plan for the risky venture of opening my own store had me very briefly dipping my toe into the swirling, roiling, dark waters of the unknown. Along with the sorrow, I experienced a palpable sense of relief.

Meanwhile, back in my job, I had been passed over for management of a larger store, and for becoming a district manager. I was also under ever mounting pressure from my employers to produce more, and more, and more, and growing weary of constantly being a referee and counselor for my employees. In my unrest, I began to re-listen to some personal growth CDs that I had acquired throughout the years. In 1999 I went to an Abraham-Hicks seminar and was the first person called to ask a question:

"How can I get out of my job?" I asked, "I am unhappy there, but don't want to leave the security."

Abraham's simple yet profound answer has blessed me ever since: "The best way to create a desired outcome is to get happy, and from that platform, you will create a happy future."

Of course! How could I get happy in circumstances that certainly didn't *feel* happy?

I did my best. I began an "Appreciation Journal", jotting down the things about my life that I enjoyed—and there were plenty—my relationship, the beauty of San Diego, and the yearly vacations we took to Hawaii. I tried to make our work environment a happy one. I had parties for my employees and guided them to better communication, making it clear that I was there to coach, not referee. I also introduced myself to the new owners of the estate jewelry store, and dropped this gem in their ear: "If you're ever going to sell the shop, please let me know!"

In 2000, Berkshire Hathaway bought the company I was working for, and I had the pleasure of having lunch (twice!) with Warren Buffett. He was unassuming and quite charming, inviting us to have our picture taken with him. He, along with the previous owners of the chain, then told us that we would be receiving a decent-sized bonus paid out over a three-year-period—how cool is THAT?!

Shortly after I had received my first bonus, opportunity #2 came knocking. "Hi Linda, we're selling our estate jewelry store, are you still interested?" There went my heart again! Out came the list of pros and cons, the calls to friends, the prayer power at church…and my conflicting thoughts. Ultimately, risking my security and losing the two future bonus payouts was just too much, especially after I found out how much they were selling the business for.

I resigned myself to spending the rest of my career in what I had labeled a stressful but do-able, familiar, and safe job. I stopped taking negative things so personally, and gained a better sense of equilibrium regardless of the situation. I did my best to focus on the positive.

I introduced myself to Gail, who, along with her jewelry-making fiancé had purchased the estate jewelry store. She was a lot of fun, and although I figured they would own the store for many years, I did mention "In case you're ever thinking about selling the store, please give me a call!"

In May of 2002, one week after I deposited the last bonus check into my savings account, I received a phone call: "Linda, my fiancé and I have separated, and I just don't want to run the shop by myself—are you still interested in buying it?"

WHAT?!?

I asked for three days to consider it, but I knew that this time my heart cartwheels led to YES!

In July, Debbie and I went to Paris on a vacation/buying trip. I had been referred to a woman there who created interesting artsy jewelry. We "clicked" immediately, and I ended up with a jewelry line for consignment at my shop. She introduced us to the wholesale jewelry district, where Debbie helped me choose treasures to sell. We also took pictures of displays, fashion, architecture, colors, and jewelry to get the creative juices flowing. I was so thankful for the "Divine Order" I was enjoying. After the whirlwind of Paris, I came home to face the enormity of my decision. What had I done?! Whenever I felt the doubts gnawing away at my confidence, I mustered my courage and moved forward anyway.

We had our quarterly manager meeting in July, and I had decided to give my notice personally to the president of the company, thinking this was the best way to deliver the news. After 22 years of dedication, it was one of the hardest things I had ever done. I was in tears a good portion of the time because it truly felt like I was leaving family. Three of the company officers came in to try to sway my decision, letting me know they did not want to lose me, which made it even harder. I was exhausted and drained when I left the corporate office, but the deed had been done. I figured I had two months to say my goodbyes, get a new manager trained, and prepare myself for my "mid-life growth spurt."

The next morning, my VP was waiting for me at the store. He accompanied me to my desk, watched while I cleaned it out, and then escorted me to the door. I was extremely shocked and shaken because what I thought was "family" turned out to be "just business." I was also getting two months less pay than I'd planned. Again, Divine Order prevailed: I was able to get unemployment and had more time to prepare for my new adventure. The experience also reminded me why I was doing this: to realize my vision of creating a company that was more than "just business," and to share love and beauty with every client.

Looking back at our lives often reveals the Grace we have experienced—both knowingly, and sometimes even in the midst of the "dark fog." My work co-exists with an insatiable thirst to know Who I Am in the spiritual sense. My career and the situations and people I encountered within it have been a vehicle for spiritual expansion and understanding.

Over the past twenty years, there have been many magical events and "coincidences" coordinated by Spirit that helped me create and launch my company:

In 1973 I had a job in Nike's accounting department. I hated the work, but I learned to wield a mean 10-key adding machine. This skill has made nearly endless inventory and paperwork at my shop a breeze.

I met a couple that happened to be liquidating their silver jewelry business, which allowed me to stock up. I was also referred to a generous vendor who agreed to lend me $100,000.00 worth of fine jewelry because of the association and longevity I had with my previous well-respected employer. I would not have been able to afford that kind of merchandise on my own. What a blessing!

A new, eight-week course on starting a business was being offered for free through the San Diego chapter of the Service Corp of Retired Executives (SCORE).

My friend Val used her extensive design acumen to help me utilize my 183 square feet of space. Several other friends helped me with various projects such as painting, cleaning, making curtains, and so on.

And perhaps the most wonderful of all…the previous owners (all of them) were more than willing to refer me to vendors, to give me whatever customer lists they had, to give me a crash course in pearl restringing, to sell me jewelry, and to get me up to speed with the quirks and delights of owning a business in La Jolla.

On Oct. 7, 2002, one day before opening, I am dressed in my scroungiest jeans after spending the day putting the final touches to the space. The moment finds me huddled in the fetal position behind one of my now beautifully adorned jewelry cases sobbing "WHAT DID I DO? I'm gonna be a bag lady!!!" After about ten minutes of the pure terror my mind was inviting me to experience, I was inspired to call Debbie, who in her wisdom was able to point me back to sanity! To this day, that moment ranks high on my "freak out" scale, and yet I have rarely felt more alive. Life invites us to move out of our comfort zone and into its' beautiful, terrifying embrace.

October 8, 2002, opening day, I am dressed in my very best "Jewels by the Sea" blue and purple ocean print dress, with matching blue shoes, purse, and eye shadow. I approach the door of my very own jewelry store, complete with a sign reading "Jewels by the Sea - Unique Jewelry and More, with prices from $5.00 - $5,000.00" and enter. The finishing touch is placing the mermaid frame (from a dear friend) enclosing the picture of smiling Warren Buffet with his arm around me, next to the cash register. With an air of accomplishment, anticipation, hesitancy, and pure joy, I take a deep breath and shout "THANK YOU GOD!" This is co-creation at its best!

ABOUT THE AUTHOR: Linda Ronelle Jalving is a Graduate Gemologist with the Gemological Institute of America, and the owner/operator of Jewels by the Sea, a unique boutique offering jewelry and gifts from $5 - $5,000. Linda transitioned from a chain jewelry store manager to a solopreneur in 2002 and considers this her "mid-life growth spurt." She encourages others to use their experiences as a source for spiritual growth. Linda serves the world through her shop, her 26 year charter membership with the San Diego Downtown Breakfast Rotary, singing at various venues, volunteering at her church, Unity San Diego, and doing her best to uplift everyone she meets.

Linda Ronelle Jalving
Jewels by the Sea - Unique Jewelry and More...from $5.00-$5,000
jewelsbythesea.biz
linda@jewelsbythesea.biz
858-459-5166

Guiding Light
Stacy Jordan Forrest

Independence Day celebrations are often filled with families and friends gathering together in parks, neighborhoods, and campgrounds. That year wasn't any different. It was mid-afternoon, July 2, 2002 when I arrived at the campground where my sister had a group campsite. My nieces and their friends were swimming in the lake, and I was catching up with family and friends who were lounging along the shore. As I was answering questions about where I was sleeping, when my husband was arriving, and so on, I noticed a man sitting near the water's edge watching the kids and listening to our conversation. As an intuitive, experienced addictions counselor who once worked with the criminal population, my inner radar kept picking up this man's energy and presence as something I needed to pay attention to. Due to my growing discomfort, we opted to leave the lake and head for the campsite.

We embarked upon our usual dinner prep, grilling and playing games prior to the anticipated campfire and marshmallow roasting. Those with an extra sweet-tooth competed to create the perfect s'more, and then bragged about how they had crafted the finest marshmallow, chocolate, and graham cracker creation.

As the moon traded places with the sun, the stars twinkled with amazing brilliance. Living in the city, one forgets just how dark the midnight sky is and what a magnificent invitation it offers the stars to be illuminated. The crackle of the fire, the midnight air, and the sound of nature brought forward such peace and tranquility. The kids had gone to bed, and my sister and I were sitting around the campfire visiting prior to going to our own tents for the night. As my brother-in-law called it a night and headed to their tent, he insisted I take a "night light" (aka glow-stick) to hang in my tent.

Being the experienced camper that I was, I refused, yet he kept insisting. To quiet him, I reluctantly accepted his offer. Little did I know, this tiny glow-stick was about to become more than simply a night light.

While we were preparing ourselves for bed, my sister asked one last time if I was sure I wanted to sleep in my tent alone, given that my husband wasn't able to come up to the campground until after work the following day. I assured her I would be fine and we said goodnight. Once in my tent, I sat on my sleeping bag and began to write in my journal, reflecting on the events of the day, thanking God for nature and family, and asking for His protection as we all slept.

Once in my sleeping bag, I turned off my flashlight and laid down. Immediately, my mind began to race with thoughts of preparation. *But for what?* I kept thinking I needed to get up and get my car keys out of the pouch that was in the pocket sewn into the corner of my tent. I heard, not audibly, but with what I call "heart thoughts", "You need to get your keys and put them next to you. You need to snap the glow-stick and hang it from the top of your tent." Though I attempted to ignore this nagging voice in my head, it would not go away. Finally, in a moment of frustration, I got out of my sleeping bag and did as I was instructed. And in truth, upon nestling back into my sleeping bag, I said, "Okay, done. Now may I go to sleep?!"

Two hours later, I woke to the sound of my sister's dog barking. My focus was immediately pulled away from the bark and toward the sound that was really in need of my attention. It was dried leaves crunching under footsteps that were walking around my tent. My heart began to race. I traced these footsteps to the corner of my tent. Staring into the dimly lit corner, I could see it being carefully pulled up. My senses were heightened. I heard, "click, click" and my mind frantically searched for the answer to what that sound was. *It's a box cutter*, I thought. *He's about to cut into my tent!* I was frozen in fear. I began to pray as never before. "Okay God, I think I'm about to die a horrible death. Please save me. What do I do?"

In that moment, as if an angel was whispering in my ear, I was told precisely what to do, and I followed every prompting. "Turn your flashlight on and let him know you are aware he is there." I slowly reached for the flashlight that was next to my shoulder and pointed it in the corner. I could hear him step back off of the plastic ground cover tarp, but he did not run or walk away. It felt like a standoff. Again I thought, *he now knows I am aware that he is there and he isn't leaving, I'm in trouble. Now what?*

Again with a steady confidence I was guided. "Slowly pick up your keys and hit the panic button." As my alarm sounded, my sister and brother-in-law came running to my rescue. My sister sat inside my tent with me while her husband, knife-in-hand, walked around my tent and surrounding area. Visibility was challenging due to the faintly lit campground. We moved my sleeping bag into their tent where my sister and I lay awake listening and looking with wide eyes and racing hearts. Upon daybreak, we went to the camp host to inform them of my petrifying event. She contacted local law enforcement who came and took my statement. The host informed the officer that she had received complaints earlier in the evening about a man that was loitering around the women's restroom and then reported that a man had left the campground first thing that morning as soon the gate opened.

Prior to this Fourth of July camping trip, I had been laid off and was rather depressed about it, even though in some ways, it seemed to be an answer to a prayer. I had been seeking divine guidance for months about leaving the company that I had grown increasingly dismayed with. My health had taken a turn for the worse due to work environment stressors. I found myself in deep despair. I'm normally the proverbial optimist and the pillar of emotional strength, but I felt I had lost the ability to tap into my inner resources and climb the ladder out of the pit I was in. Days before the camping trip, I had told my husband that I hoped being out in nature would help my depression because I felt so lost I didn't care if I lived or died. I knew something needed to change.

On that summer's eve, I believe I was given the opportunity to live or die. I was offered the option of listening and acting, of fighting to save my life, or of releasing the struggles of this world and leaving. Even now as I write, my heart is overwhelmed at the thought. We have a God who really does listen, who cares for us and is ever-present in our struggles and times of need. Divine love is the most beautiful love. We, in our human limitations, cannot fully comprehend the pureness and availability of such love. If only we could embrace this truth, we would live lives of free abandon, conquering our fears and negative messaging. We would be free from limitations imposed by ourselves and others, and we would love from a place that is deep and authentic.

The question is "HOW?" In my current work as a therapist, I hear this often. "I know that would be better for me, but *how* do I find this place of peace, contentment and love?" In my nineteen years working as a healer, I have sat with many suffering souls and I have seen the desperation in their eyes. I hear the cries of their hearts and the longing to be free. With compassion, I gaze upon each of these beings and I say, "Live in grace and gratitude." Initially, this is not easy. But it is essential. We are all here to extend and receive grace, to forgive and be forgiven, and to love as we are loved. I believe this is the lesson we are here to live out, experience, and learn. Each one of us is offered numerous lessons along our life's path. Our journey is rich with peaks and valleys, deserts and daisy fields. I have seen the soul's winter and the hope of spring. There is life even in the lifeless seasons. We are to embrace the journey with anticipation for the next season, because it always comes, though we may not see or sense it. Faithful is the promise of tomorrow.

During my camping trauma I decided to choose life. Though I was forever changed in that terrifying moment, I was alive. God had a plan and I was going to move into it. I returned to school to continue my education and earned a Bachelor and a Master's degree, and moved into a higher gifting and calling in my life. I decided then that I would no longer live as if I were dying, but rather *eagerly await the unfolding* (my newly adopted motto) of all that is divinely designed for my life. And in so doing, I have been blessed with miracle moments.

For example, in 2005 I woke from a dream that was so clear I felt I had to draw it (now mind you, I am no artist). So, in the prayer journal I kept, I drew out in detail this dream of a building that was someday supposed to be a Wellness Center. It had a huge wrap-around front porch and an A-frame roofline. I drew all the specific details, including exactly how the inside looked. For years, whenever my husband and I would drive by a similar-looking property, I would light-heartedly say, "I wonder if that's supposed to be our Wellness Center."

In July of 2010, my husband and I were looking at spaces because I needed to move my office. We drove by an older home that had a wrap-around porch and an A-frame front, and I said my typical mantra. Yet as we passed this property, I felt something different than usual. It felt as if something hit my chest. With a racing heart, I yelled, "Stop the car!" We parked and walked around the building. We met with the realtor and toured it. The moment I entered, I just knew I had been there before, even though I had not. It was very familiar to me. I looked at my husband and said, "I think this is it, this is my dream." We went home to find my journal. My husband located it and called for me to quickly come, for he could hardly believe his own eyes. There was my drawing, detailing every aspect of this property: pane windows, hallway, lobby location, my office with the fireplace, everything right down to the specific colors on the walls.

In reflection, I see many lessons presented as trials. On that traumatic Independence Day so long ago, I learned to hold on to hope, even though I couldn't see a way forward. I believed in God's plan, even though I didn't understand it. And through the years, I remained faithful and open to possibilities, and fully embraced a future I had only once dreamed of. With perseverance and partnership, we have a thriving Health & Wellness Center that has been helping to transform lives for the past six years.

I frequently hear clients' comment as they enter the lobby, remarking on how they experience tranquility as well as sense the presence of divine light and love. Upon completion of services, one of my clients gifted me with a beautiful glass picture of our wooden Craftsman lobby door, and inscribed on the glass were these words: *This is where the healing begins. Where darkness meets the light.*

Along my journey, I have come to realize that Grace is a gift and Gratitude is the response. It's the spiritual "Thank you" we extend from a grateful heart.

ABOUT THE AUTHOR: Stacy Jordan Forrest LPC, NCC, CADC, BCLC is an intuitive mental health therapist and spiritual life coach who is passionate about facilitating healing, restoration and transformation in her clients' lives. Stacy has nineteen years of experience working in the mental health field counseling, teaching and consulting. She established Entheos Health & Wellness Center in Oregon City, where she has her private practice. Stacy holds a master's degree in counseling, a bachelor's degree in human development, is certified as an alcohol and drug counselor and holds certificates in women's issues, eating disorders, marriage, and life coaching. In her free time she enjoys spending time with her family, God and nature.

Stacy Jordan Forrest LPC, NCC, CADC, BCLC
New Beginnings Counseling Services
entheoswellnesscenter.com
stacyforrest@comcast.net
971-506-1885

A New Beginning
Martha Venditto

As a child of divorced parents, I grew up in a house with three generations. There were my grandparents, my mom, my aunt and uncle. Being the only child in the house I was spoiled, but I was also taught that I had to earn whatever I wanted. Watching all the musicals on the four o'clock movies made me believe in happily ever after.

Someday I will marry and have children, a house, a dog and a cat. I dream of the white wedding dress and the big party, the honeymoon in Hawaii. I graduate high school and start working in the local department store. I meet a guy who is handsome, dark-eyed, dark-haired—my dream guy. He works in the stock area. He thinks I'm standoffish, maybe I am. By spring we are dating; by summer we are engaged, with the wedding set for the following summer. Yes, I have the big Italian wedding with all the trimmings. My mother spares no expense, and it's everything I'd dreamed off. Off to Hawaii we go.

We have two children, the house, the dog and the cat. Holidays are spent together with family and friends. Summertime is spent barbequing and making wine. Vacations were plenty, Italy, California, Alaska, Bermuda just to name a few places. Each one feels like it is our honeymoon.

Many of those vacations are paid for by me. When the kids are small I am fortunate enough to be able to stay home with them, but eventually I start hearing, "Maybe you should get a job. "You need to bring money into the house." So when our youngest is eight I get a job with a local financial institution. It is a little intimidating to be back in the workforce after so many years, but it feels good too. I do well there and over the years I receive promotion after promotion and am eventually made branch manager. I am excited; I am proud of myself. I think this is only the beginning; my husband thinks it is the end. "Don't take any more promotions," he tells me, "You don't need to work. Why you are going for that position?" It is like he's afraid I will make more money than him. I don't listen though, and go on to become a second VP at the bank. Once again I am thrilled. Then the bank merges with another, giving me the opportunity to work in the main office and experience a host of benefits while continuing to grow my career. He does not support this, so it's back to being a branch manager. In the meantime, my paycheck continues to pay for all the good things in life—vacations, hobbies (loved the motorcycle rides) and all things you can do when your children are grown and out of the house.

In the meantime, I support his dreams. He has a city job but he really wants to own his own business. And he tries them all—he sells used cars, has a Mr. Fixit, and considers opening a laundromat. The next to last venture is a concession supply wholesale that he owns with a friend. It does well, but there always seems to be more going out than coming in. Then, after ten years, he decides to call it quits and lets the partner have everything. So another refinance of the mortgage for another business—this time a cold storage facility with my cousin. This one is "the one," he says, except that it isn't. Eventually the business folds and we are left with a large mortgage—too much to sustain on his salary from the city. And still I support and love him.

Our daughter and son are close to each other. One lies and the other swears to it. If I had a sibling (that lived close by) this is how I would want the relationship to be. So our son introduces his sister to his best friend and before we all realize it there is a wedding. What a beautiful day. We are the parents of the bride. Our first grandchild is born two years later. What pride and joy a grandchild brings. We are grandparents for the first time.

My son, who has been dating the same girl for about six years, announces that they are buying a house and getting married; just imagine the excitement of another wedding. In the midst of all this, our daughter and son-in-law are expecting their second child.

As a married couple, my husband and I had the usual squabbles, spats and misunderstandings. But I never expect the huge argument that erupts one day in the spring of 2010, shortly before our son's wedding. My husband is angry about a loan I had taken out against my 401K, so angry in fact that he moves out of our bedroom. I am completely shocked, especially since I had taken out the loan to help pay for the wedding! I spend two months in a state of confused limbo, until he finally says the words I've been dreading: "I want a divorce. You spent all our money."

Even as my world crumbles around me I say, "You can get your divorce. I'm not going to make it easy and let's be truthful, you have a girlfriend."

The words you have a girlfriend come out of my mouth so quickly I don't even realize what I've said until I look into his eyes, those beautiful brown eyes. We are one month short of our thirty-fourth wedding anniversary. Happy anniversary to me.

I am served with divorce papers at my neighbor's Labor Day barbeque, with her whole family looking on. Two weeks later, me and my soon-to-be-ex are at the wedding; when it's time to announce the groom's parents, it's not "Mr. and Mrs.," but our first names. All day long his phone rings, and although he has admitted to nothing, the sinking feeling in my gut tells me exactly who it is.

Completely crushed, I fight the urge to hide and instead hold my head up high at each court date. Six months into the divorce proceedings the girlfriend is finally revealed. Not a younger woman, and not a stranger either, but a neighbor. He has already introduced her to his mother, sister and brother-in-law at a holiday dinner. Even worse, all the other neighbors know about her too. Talk about being the last to know. Again, I walk with my head held high, and remember my grandmother's words, "Always be a lady, always walk with grace."

For the next two years I struggle with loneliness and pennilessness—I don't know what is worse. I have to pay for half the household bills, (mortgage, electric, gas, homeowners insurance), plus my own cell phone, car insurance, health insurance, and other personal expenses. My credit cards, which my husband and I had used primarily for vacations, is now what I'm living on. I'd always had the better credit score, but given my inability to pay on time, that soon changes. Between the pain of the divorce and the financial stress, I feel like I'm drowning.

The worst part is having no one to talk to. My mother passed away and I am an only child. I can't talk to my own children, for that would be pitting them against their father. Finally, I admit I need help. Every week for the next three years I pour my heart out to a social worker/psychiatrist; it is the best thing I have done for myself since I can't remember when.

I also find a women's organization called Powerful You!, which turns out to be a real catalyst for change in my life. At the end of each meeting, when we do the "gratitude share," I start to realize all the good in my life, how fortunate I am.

Journaling is another powerful practice I adopt during the divorce. Each day I write down my thoughts and reflections on what has happened. But the real healing occurs through my volunteer work with various organizations and non-profits, something I had done even before my husband left. In memory of a co-worker, I volunteer with the local Chapter of the American Cancer Society. I do the Making Strides Breast Cancer walk, the Spring Gala, and Relay for Life. I am engaged with the world again and enjoying the good I am doing.

A month after our son's wedding, and with the pain of the divorce still raw, I receive a phone call from the head of the Staten Island Chapter of the American Cancer Society. I am to be named Volunteer of the Year at the Spring Gala! It means so much to me that all the work I had done is being recognized. Yet, as the night of the Gala approaches I find myself lonely, confused, and upset. *How do I get through this? My husband is supposed to enjoy this honor with me.*

Instead, I get something better: an outpouring of support I could never have imagined. My mother-in-law, sister-in-law, and brother-in-law are there, along with my children, their spouses, and my aunt and her companion. Also in attendance are my supervisor from the bank and nine of my co-workers; longtime friends, new friends, and business members from the Staten Island Business Council networking group. I am loved and I feel it. My name is called, and my son escorts me as I walk up to receive my award. In that moment something comes over me. It isn't fear, it isn't anxiety, and it isn't even the thought of being alone. At that moment I feel the strength to carry on; I am becoming my own person. I am being recognized for helping others, and this is empowering to me. I am doing something that I enjoy.

In May of 2011 I am asked to join Soroptimist International, a service organization dedicated to helping women and girls around the world. As I sit at a new member meeting and listen to the facilitator talk about things like human trafficking, domestic violence, and obstacles to getting an education, I realize I am not that bad off. Each day I take baby steps; I find a place to live, I make a new home for myself. I live with strength, and grace and independence. Two apartments later, I am happy. I control my own destiny. I travel with the different organizations to their respective conferences and conventions. My children need a calendar to see where I'll be on a given day.

I understand how devastating it is going through the divorce process. It is a lonely time. Your family doesn't know what to say to you. They are angry at the spouse. Your friends try not to take sides but you are the third wheel at the dinner table. This is some of what I had experienced, and I make a vow to help others through the process. There is much gratitude and fulfillment knowing I can help others. When the divorce becomes final I start a non-profit 501c3 organization called S.E.L.F. Stand Empowered Live Free. The mission statement is *to inspire women and men that they can continue through their life during the divorce process. To support each one to accomplish their goals as they go into a new phase of their life. To ensure that they are important, to Stand Empowered, Live Free.*

It has been six years since that day in 2010 when I was asked for the divorce. I have retired from my job and am enjoying every minute of my life. I volunteer with Kiwanis International Richmond County club, The Dr. Theodore A. Atlas Foundation, Soroptimist International of Americas Staten Island Club, The Salvation Army, and Protecting One Young Heart at a Time in memory of Frank J Reali III. Each one of these non-profit organizations fills my life with good, strength, courage, and gratitude that I can help out in any way I can.

To quote Helen Reddy, "I am strong, I am invincible, I am woman." Each day I thank the universe for all the good in my life. As I am able to be thankful for all that I have, I receive more and more into my life, and I am whole.

ABOUT THE AUTHOR: Martha Venditto is an author, advocate, mother and grandmother, and former finance executive. Born into a traditional New York Italian family, she was raised by her mother, aunt, uncle, and grandparents, until she married at age twenty. During her twenty-seven-year career in finance, she had the opportunity to volunteer for various non-profit organizations, many of which benefit women and girls, both across the country and around the world. She currently serves on the Salvation Army Advisory Board and belongs to the Dr. Theodore A Atlas Foundation, Kiwanis, and Soroptimist International. She is also the founder of S.E.L.F.—Stand Empowered Live Free, a non-profit organization that assists people going through a divorce.

Martha C Venditto
Retired banker
32mvenditto@gmail.com
917-837-1589

Coming Home
Tracy Carlson

"Home is a place we all must find, child. It's not just a place where you eat or sleep. Home is knowing. Knowing your mind, knowing your heart, knowing your courage. If we know ourselves, we're always home, anywhere." ~ Glinda the Good Witch, *The Wizard of Oz*

I love the movie The Wizard of Oz for its brilliant use of metaphor. Storms may brew in our lives—addiction, loss, sickness—and everything flies apart. Suddenly we aren't in Kansas anymore and, like Dorothy and her companions, are forced down the yellow brick road of spiritual awakening—that journey home to our own heart.

It sounds so easy—just know yourself and you're always home, anywhere. It is easy, unless you decide it's going to be hard. For me, getting to know myself seemed like a heroic task, fraught with peril. The hardest thing I've ever done, I think, is to learn to accept and love myself completely, especially the dark, ugly parts. The parts that seemed broken and scary and dangerous, like hideous flying monkeys seeking to rip out my stuffing and carry me away unless I surrender.

Getting to know myself has been a vulnerable process, a courageous journey fueled by a deep longing for spiritual connection and healing. It has required a willingness to feel pain, to learn true gratitude—to be grateful for everything just as it is—and to accept the gift of grace in which I discovered permission to love and be loved, just as I am.

Gifts of Grace

It is a brilliant, sky blue, puffy-cloud day in June. The sun is jubilant, the breeze is just the right shade of cool, and I am standing in the exact spot in the hospital parking lot where I remember standing when I was three years old, and looking up at the exact fourth floor window I looked up at then. It's a poignant moment for me. The hospital is now abandoned and broken windows have been boarded up. Twisted poplar seedlings, thistles and wild prairie grass have grown up over the emergency entrance, like Sleeping Beauty's castle after a hundred years of enchanted slumber. I have been attending a professional meeting in a building next door, and during a break I felt inexplicably drawn to this spot.

As I gaze up at that window, a veil is lifted. Suddenly I am that three year-old again, standing beside my grandma and grandpa. Grandma is pointing up to the window, making sure I see my mother. I burst into tears because she has been away so long and I'm not allowed in the hospital to visit. Grandpa kneels down on one knee behind me and just holds me as I cry. He doesn't try to fix anything—he just lets me know he is there. He provides a grace-filled presence for me—the physical experience of a loving father—and somehow I know that I am not alone. I am safe and everything I need is always right here, right where I am, no matter what seems to be happening around me.

Gifts of Gratitude

Alcoholism has been a constant companion of mine for as long as I can remember. Indeed, it has been at the root of every deeply painful experience I've ever had. It's a spiritual disease—and a lonely one—whether you are the drinker or the one who loves a drinker, or some combination of the two. It's quite extraordinary to now be in a space of profound gratitude in the experience of alcoholism. Alcoholism brought me to my knees, where, as the saying goes, I should have been all along.

When I was about eight years old my cousin and I got stuck in the cab of my uncle's new tractor. We'd been playing in the barnyard and it was just too tempting to pass up. At first it was great fun—we poked around at all the buttons and pretended we were driving—but when it came time to get out, we couldn't open the door. We tried the handles, then banged on the windows, and within minutes were screaming and crying in sheer terror. It was strange, really, like each of us forgot we had each other; we forgot we weren't alone. After what seemed like hours of raging, we had finally spent ourselves. As quiet fell over the cab, we decided to pray for help. Within minutes, my uncle appeared and opened the door. Apparently he had been working in the barnyard the whole time but never heard us as we screamed and cried and banged on the windows. It was only when we got quiet and prayed for help that he "heard" us.

Living with alcoholism is like being a child stuck in a tractor. If you don't let go, calm yourself, and ask for help from your Higher Power, you might be in there for a very long time.

Flash forward to middle age, when I found myself laying— metaphorically speaking—in the middle of the road with an emotional sucking chest wound, and people were stepping over me and walking around me, smiling, asking, "How are you?"

And I would smile back, oh so brightly, and respond with the obligatory, "Fine," all the while feeling invisible.

In reality, I was the opposite of fine. It seemed as though everything in my life was falling apart—my marriage, my business, my finances, and I felt as though I couldn't breathe. Feelings of terror and hopelessness, regret and self-loathing consumed me; I could not sleep, I could not eat. An emotional storm was raging inside me, and I could not find a port to ride it out in. I was in a place of complete undoing, a very dangerous place indeed. Yet somehow I knew that I was being called out by a power much greater than me to stop living in circumstance and to step into a greater version of myself.

I discovered that the greatest spiritual gifts often come wrapped in the most loathsome packaging—death, divorce, alcoholism—and are usually tied up with thick ribbons of fear. For so many years I refused to accept these gifts; thinking of them as curses I instead buried them and pretended they didn't exist. When they surfaced, I fought against them. I stomped on them, I tried to give them away to others, or I tried to hide them in the closet. It took a complete undoing of my inner and outer world to force me to stop and have a good look at them. I was determined to see things differently and to accept responsibility for my own life, at last.

When I stopped running from my problems, stopped trying to fix them, and faced my pain, something quite extraordinary occurred. I found the eye of the storm. Right in the middle of all the chaos there was a calm, quiet, and peaceful place inside of me. It was from that place that I was able to face the carnage that was my life. Eventually I began to hear that still, small voice, and I found the grace to love and forgive myself. I arrived at the knowing that I have a sacred responsibility to complete myself, to come home to God, whose consciousness resides in me, even when I'm too busy suffering to feel it or hear it. It took courage to stay with it, but once the fearsome wrappings were discarded I was delighted with what was inside: unconditional love, authentic freedom, and the joy that naturally springs forth from a grateful heart.

A Place We All Must Find

"We shall not cease from explorations, and the end of all our exploring will be to arrive where we started and know the place for the first time."
~T.S. Eliot

This journey of mine has required a willingness to walk a little slower, embrace my pain, practice self-forgiveness, and to present myself to God, just as I am. I realize that all those broken pieces of my life—those things that I spent years secretly trying to piece back together—were meant to be broken so that something more beautiful, truthful, and joyful could be created from the rubble. My spiritual journey has been a decision to set forth with faith on that yellow brick road of spiritual awakening, link arms with the people who show up for me, and to go forth in joy.

I am done with making plans on my own, with trying to navigate this life blindly—I don't do life without the anointing. I know that I have an Inner Guide who is far wiser than me, who is always whispering in my ear what step to take next on this path that I have chosen. As Gandhi said, it's a voice that is as loud as my willingness to hear. And so I simply brush off distraction and discouragement and behave like a sunflower—keeping my face turned toward the light. Knowing that God walks with me on my path gives me strength and a boldness I have never experienced before.

"You shall know the truth, and the truth shall set you free." ~ John 8:32

I am so grateful for my grandpa on that long ago day in June, holding me as I stood in the hospital parking lot, crying and gazing forlornly at my mother. It was this experience of a loving father that kept me so cognizant—and so connected—with a power greater than myself. Grandpa provided the container for me to experience the knowing that I am never alone, even if circumstances make it appear otherwise. I am loved, I am safe, and all my needs are perfectly met. If I hadn't had the memory of that experience, what would have happened? I might have given up. I might have been swept away in the storm. I might not have found my way home.

Now, when the storm of circumstance is brewing, the sky has turned black, the wind is howling I head for home. All it really takes is a slow, deep breath, a willingness to embrace the pain—remaining profoundly grateful for the lessons in it—and accepting the grace that is available in every moment to lift me up on wings, through the dark clouds and above where the sky is blue and the sun is always shining. With a click of my heels, I am home, where everything is always in right and perfect order, *no matter what.*

ABOUT THE AUTHOR: Tracy Carlson is a certified transformational life coach, as well as a registered social worker specializing in clinical counseling. She is an educator, mentor, counselor, program developer, speaker, workshop facilitator and author. Tracy resides in Saskatoon, Saskatchewan, Canada, where she enjoys music, art, culture and meandering along the river trails. She loves spending time with her family, cuddling grandbabies, sharing belly laughs with friends, and engaging in conversations about things that matter with people who care.

Tracy Carlson
Out of the Blue Life SOULutions
outofthebluetherapy.ca
tracy@outofthebluetherapy.ca
306-747-5985

See Jane Run
Jane Moresco

When I was young, I was so busy running through life that I didn't pay attention or stop... that is, until I finally flat-lined and was brought to my knees by tragedy. It happened on February 12, 2002—that my twenty-one-year-old son took his own life.

Even though that day was over fourteen years ago, I can tell you exactly what I was wearing, what I did and who I was with.

Up until that day, I had lived through some tough stuff and survived, but this... How was I going to keep it together and get up from this? *Oh God, help me*, I thought, but looking back I think He had been preparing me. As someone once said, "Mary lost her son too." Reflecting on those words actually made me feel peaceful and reminded me that I wasn't the only one going through this grief. Someone else had experienced it as well.

Grief is the conflicting feelings caused by the end of or a change in a familiar pattern of behavior. Grief is normal and a natural emotional reaction to loss or change of any kind, and I had experienced loss and change before...

349 Manor Avenue

Throughout my growing up years, I had always thought of myself as privileged and lucky. My life wasn't too shabby. Oh, our family had our problems and issues, but growing up with a mom, a dad, and two older brothers in a large home with two gardeners and a housekeeper two days a week, was pretty good. I had a family that was well-connected in the community, had lots of social life, and always had company. You get the picture...yep, things were good... that is, until my parents died four months apart when I was only nineteen.

I remember thinking, *Oh my God, this wasn't supposed to*

happen to us. I thought we were exempt! My parents were good people who did charity work and provided well for our family. After this happened, my life was a blur because I was so busy trying to stay afloat and not fall for fear of not getting up. I didn't realize that those feelings were grief knocking on my door...

So what did I do next? I went ahead and got married to the man who is the love of my life and who has been with me through it all. We had been planning our wedding even before my parents died.

778 McKenzie Street

The house on McKenzie Street was our first home as a married couple. Our daughter and son were born there. It was two blocks from my parents' home and a block from his parents' home. This was a small community where everyone knew everyone and all about them. It was a great place to grow up and a great place to have kids.

My husband went to work every day and I stayed home to do the "kids thing." I took them to school, baseball, and dance. I did charity work and all the stuff my parents had taught me to do by the time I was nineteen.

When the kids were three and five, we rented out the McKenzie Street house and moved a few blocks away, but I would return to this home, our first home, after our son died, to heal, and to try to put one foot in front of the other.

594 Vivienne Drive

The new house on Vivienne Drive was the home that we primarily raised our kids in. That house hosted birthday parties, first communions, holidays, and sleepovers.

I always went into my son Greg's room to say goodbye in the mornings, but on the morning of the day he died, I didn't do that. I wasn't mad at him; I was just letting him sleep, not waking him up, "giving him his space."

I had been working on giving people their space because I had realized that somewhere along the line, I had become a control freak. I wanted to keep everyone safe and I didn't trust that they were capable of doing that for themselves. When that control thing is not going well, it feels like a runaway freight train that you can't stop. I desperately wanted the train to stop. *STOP and let me off!*

So, step one: Don't bug your son...Well, how did that work? Not well that day! Oh God, how were we going to go on without Greg?

I had always kept myself so busy, just running through life and not dealing with life changes, but this time I knew I would either sink and flat-line or stand up. I chose to stand up. *I'll take stand up for 200 dollars!*... but how?

...

By the time Greg died, I had been listening to Joel Osteen, Joyce Meyer, and Oprah for a while and practicing being grateful. I was in my forties and I felt like my life was in shambles. I remember thinking, "I can't do this anymore, but maybe if I surrender to God, that will work." So standing in front of the mirror, I said "Okay God, I surrender."

I felt really stupid, but instantly I started to notice things were shifting for me. I slowed down and got quiet; I went from manic to peaceful. I felt like I was in slow motion, lethargic... but it was working and I liked it!

Now, I could live in the moment, and when I did, it was peaceful. I was opening to blessings and becoming stronger, and when I talked to people, I was focused on them; my mind wasn't all over the place. I started to practice saying something nice to whoever I was talking to, you know the thoughts that you have but don't verbalize, like, "I love your hair," or "I love your shoes." I would look for something, say it, and then I would say to myself, "Wow this feels good." It always would make me smile. I was grateful for my life.

I also knew there was a message here. The message was that I was an example. I couldn't depend on others to hold me up; it was up to me to do it for myself, even if all the while my other voice was saying, "God, do I have to? Oh my God, isn't there an easier way? I just need time off. Let me breathe... please!" But each time this would happen, I would pull myself together and focus on the moment at hand.

My interaction with God had gone this way for some time, with me asking for relief from my pain and God delivering it experientially. Then one day, something shifted; God and I had what could definitely be described as a two-way chat. Have you ever had a whisper that keeps whispering? It is inside your head and yet you know it is originating from somewhere—or someone—else. It is both surreal and yet the "realest" thing one can ever feel. My whisper went something like this:

"Oh, good morning, God! Is that you? Okay, God, yes, I hear you... Yes, I know I'm here to help others... But I'm a *realtor*!... No, I know I can't just sit back when I have conquered all that's been... Oh, look into going to coaching school?... But I'm supposed to go to a real estate seminar. Yes, I feel like that would be interesting... But what will I tell my family? They'll think I've lost my mind! Yes, of course I love helping people with real estate... I know... yes, this is helping people move through and get to the other side of something, like grief, that is holding them back... Sure, I can help others with that... HELLO!... Are you sure, God?... It's just hard to figure out what I'm supposed to do and trust that it's the right path..."

Later, it was: "Hey, guess what, God?... I finished coaching school... Oh, it's not quite the right time... oh, start with the story and the rest will follow... Okay, God... Hey, are You sure this is You?... Are You sure I have what it takes?... Okay... Okay... I'll trust You and if it falls into place and moves in the direction of coaching others through grief then I'll know for sure You are guiding me..."

Then it hit me—I already *knew* I was being guided by God. I had already created the grievewithgracecoaching.com website, and was going to be a contributor to this book. The realization that things were indeed moving forward inspired me to do even more to help others heal their grief. This encompassed not only grief over the loss of a person, but the loss of a relationship, a job... some people even grieve a huge weight loss and the person they used to be. Or maybe they are just plain stuck and are grieving the time they lost in their life.

"Okay, okay, I got this, God!... Oh and one more thing... Thank You God... For all of it!"

Now, looking back over the years, it is pretty empowering to see what I have accomplished and survived. It's almost surreal, but I'm proud and grateful. I finally see what people meant when they told me, "The best is yet to come." Now, it has!

Through my divinely-guided process of slowing down and calming myself, I have become better able to listen to other people as they speak about their struggles. They have told me that I'm very intuitive and have provided them with tools that helped them see situations from a different perspective and effect a more positive outcome. It doesn't get much better than that!

It is with both grace and gratitude, however, that I have been able to move past that grief. Each day my heart is overflowing with gratitude for my family, friends, and the community that cared so much for my wellbeing, and that gratitude has made me realize that I wanted to be there for them as they were there for me. Gratitude for my son's life, as short as it was, has allowed me to keep him alive in ways I would have never imagined. Yes, I can say the best is yet to come... and to think I would have missed it if I hadn't fought so hard to live myself.

Even the darkest night will end and the sun will rise. ~ Victor Hugo

As I look back at my journey, I'm reminded of a special place our family and some friends have vacationed over the years. It's in the mountains, and we stay in rustic cabins and swim at the pool that hasn't changed in forty-plus years. There are trails to hike, creeks to crawdad fish in, and deer and wild turkey to watch in all their beauty. One day, as I stood on the bridge and observed the flowing creek, it occurred to me—this creek was like life, running gracefully along until some obstacle causes it to pool in one spot. And just when it seems it will always be there, growing stagnant, it overflows and flows forth again toward all the goodness nature has to offer.

Grace is both a manner of movement that is smooth and not awkward as well as unmerited divine assistance given to us humans. To grieve with grace is about finding acceptance with how things are being unfolded in a way where you can learn to embrace loss as a blessing, meant to help us grow and become stronger. Grieving with grace is about facing the loss that challenges us to change and become a more powerful version of ourselves.

ABOUT THE AUTHOR: Jane Moresco is no stranger to grief. At nineteen, she lost both parents and her grandmother in rapid succession. Years later, tragedy struck again when a close friend passed away, followed by her brother. But it was her son's suicide at the age of twenty-one that finally led her to confront the pent-up pain and anguish. She came to see grief as a gift that can help us break down walls, create more intimate relationships and allow the blessings of life to fall naturally into place. Today, Jane is a Certified Professional Coach, and ELI-MP (Energy Leadership Master Practitioner). In her practice, Grieve with Grace Coaching, she opens a space for others to embrace their grief and move into healing.

Jane Moresco CPC, ELI-MP
Certified Life Coach
grievewithgracecoaching.com
Janemoresco@yahoo.com
831-254-0852

Grace, Gratitude, & Orgasms
Linda Albright

"They're all inside you," he whispered. "Hundreds of them—thousands perhaps—just waiting to come out. We just need to go get them."

Those were the wise words of the Divine Shaman Lover I had attracted into my life at age fifty. In an instant, he knew that what I'd been chasing my whole life —pleasure, fulfillment, release, in a word orgasm—was lodged deep within me. Up until then I had just assumed I was incapable of true satisfaction, like I'd been born with a factory defect that I should just learn to live with. Of course I'd had orgasms before, but never regularly, and rarely with my caring and kind partners. And I certainly had never experienced anything like Meg Ryan's timeless impersonation in *When Harry Met Sally*. "Is that for REAL?!" I wondered quietly to myself for years.

For years I had chased the Holy Orgasm Grail, and kept looking to the outside to scratch that interminable itch. Playful romps, drunken escapades, steamy nightclub bathroom scenes—all done in search of the wholeness and satisfaction I'd heard was possible. (Only in retrospect do I see the folly of this methodology!) I figured I just needed to *try harder, get out there more, make it happen*. And while I became quite adept at pleasing whatever male flavor of the month I was with (okay, admittedly, not hard to do), I was always left wanting, wondering, and assuming *there's just something wrong with **me.***

The Over-Achiever that I am, I'd made heroic efforts to solve my problem at midlife. In fact, when I met Michael, I had just invested 18K in a real-life training program whose sole purpose was to teach women how to unleash the inner goddess, to release the Divine feminine energy that apparently was the Magic Key to our happiness, success, and power. All that would be great, I thought, but really, secretly, *I just wanted to learn how to get off with a man in the room.*

See, as a good little New England WASP, with an Ivy League education and more schooling than I could fit on a business card, I had spent my fifty years following "The Rules." I had built successful businesses, launched impactful community projects, and managed a high-functioning family with all the trimmings. I ran a marathon, drank protein shakes, and even volunteered on First Grade Library Days. I had masterminded a massive, cross-country family move and secured a gorgeous five-thousand-square-foot classic Tudor home with a flowing stream in the backyard, which I could hear through the windows of my professionally-designed bedroom. I absolutely HAD IT ALL. Money. Family. Business. Health. Friends. The Ultimate American Dream.

But orgasms—those wild, unruly pleasure pockets—were nowhere to be found.

Somehow my proven, unconscious mantra of "Do More! Work Harder!" didn't quite translate in the bedroom or generate the multiple, mind-blowing orgasms I'd heard about. What was a Can-Do-Girl to do?

When we first met, Michael didn't buy my sexual façade for a second. Almost six feet tall, and attractive by most standards, I had used my sexuality to both my business and personal advantage my entire life—I figured if you got it, use it, even if, ironically, it rarely led to sexual satisfaction. I didn't abuse my sexual prowess, but rather employed it just enough to give me a leg up in male-dominated sales meetings, or to get a free drink at the bar. Michael instantly saw through that first line of defense, and knew intuitively that hiding behind all that bravado and all that accomplishment was an undeveloped, untrusting, and unsatisfied little girl.

And so the messy process began.

Lest you think this was a path of roses, romance, and wild passionate release, think again. Yes, there was plenty of exploration and ecstasy, but alongside that was intense fighting, iron-clad resistance, and full throttle railing against the whole darn thing. Because what he was "forcing" me to do—which was, God forbid, *enjoy my life*—was *counter to everything I knew that worked.* I'm an indoctrinated work horse, a performer. When I met him, my life was chopped up into well-constructed categories, each managed with NASA precision; I even had the color-coded electronic calendar to prove it. So there was NO ROOM for lounging, adventure, or exploration, because those required that valuable commodity called TIME which needed to be spent watching kids on a ballfield, schmoozing at business meetings, or quietly meditating by my stream. How could *my pleasure* possibly be of equal rank, let alone take priority over those? Play and pleasure? Ha. That's what the non-serious, unaccomplished set do. "I am woman, hear me ROAR!" I railed...not whimper from behind bedroom walls, for cryin' out loud.

Phew. My poor guy had his work cut out for him.

Essentially, we began the sloppy job of turning not just my sexual life—but the WHOLE ENCHILADA—on its head. And I learned that it not only required time, but things even more precious: trust, vulnerability, communication, patience. None of which I even remotely knew how to do. YIKES. If that wasn't enough to send me packing...

But I stayed. And learned. And opened up. And trusted...and was rewarded with steamy scenes I swore existed only in Danielle Steele novels. Turns out that toe-curling, back-arching stuff IS REAL, ladies.

Through that messy, intense, and seemingly dangerous process, I not only found the path and joy of orgasm, I also found an equally priceless prize: a new way to live my life, which affects everything—business, parenting, health, money, and partnership. The "Push! Push! Push!" approach that ran my life is slowly being replaced by the "Relax...Receive...Attract...Invite...Revel" one. I now better understand that the juicy things in life I don't *make happen*; I *allow them to*. The Doer in me will never die, but she's been joined by a calmer, wiser Elder who understands that's only half of the equation. And now, if I find myself in a place where I just "don't have time" to enjoy all my beautiful creations—my vibrant children, beautiful home, exceptional clients, or gorgeous hunk of a man—then it's crystal clear that *I'm living my life backwards*.

What I realized was that underneath it all was a fundamental imbalance in my system. I realized I'd been living my life from the neck up—essentially, walking around as a disembodied, floating head. I needed to find balance, not between the PTA and the Chamber of Commerce, but between Mind, Body, Soul and Spirit. I needed to own my own shadow and embrace all of the parts I'd disowned and had learned to hide and deny quite well. My mind had to start working *for me* instead of trying to hijack my life. I had to live in and care for my Body Temple. I had to bring my Soul and Spirit into bed with me. Only then could I experience those life-changing moments where time stops while my Mind/Body/Spirit meld with not only my partner but with Consciousness itself.

All I can say is that Grace provided me this life lesson by connecting me to my Shaman Lover on a random online dating site one lonely Saturday night, all alone in my well-appointed bedroom. And since that fateful introduction, I'm learning to not only *accept* joy and pleasure, I'm actually figuring out how to live my life and accomplish things without the persistent hunger that always pushed me further, faster, harder. Quite frankly, I miss that girl sometimes, the one who only had one speed—GO!—and so things were actually simpler back then. I've definitely lost my Get-Things-Done Edge, the thing that pushed me forward in my younger days, but in its stead is a grounded, satisfied woman whose thirst—believe it or not—has finally, and undeniably, been quenched. If that's not Grace, I don't know what is.

How's the story end?

Well my Shaman Lover and I are about to celebrate our one-year anniversary, even though our relationship by most measures *should not work*. What are the odds that a suburban entrepreneur with three teenagers and a crackpot dad under her roof could successfully match up with a rock-climbing, Empty Nester who's aching to sail the world on his vintage wooden schooner? Oh, and did I mention we live ninety minutes apart?

And yet it works, thank goodness, due to a deep alignment and commitment to plumbing the depths of the Body/Mind/Spirit connection, together, while the hunt for the next few hundred continues….

ABOUT THE AUTHOR: Women's Wealth Revolution™ founder Linda Albright believes financially and spiritually empowered women make the world stronger, healthier and happier. For that reason she is passionate about helping heart-centered visionaries reclaim their confidence, align their spirituality with their business mission, and create abundance. After decades building successful businesses, Linda founded and grew her own multi-six-figure company. She serves on the Advisory Board of the national networking group Over 40 Females, and is a Founding Board Member of the Copper Beech Institute, a center for mindfulness in Connecticut. She also spends time marveling over her aging body, three hormonal teenagers, and feisty octogenarian father. Never a dull day in the Albright house.

Linda Albright
Women's Wealth Revolution
womenswealthrevolution.com
Linda@womenswealthrevolution.com
facebook.com/WomensWealthRevolution

Living from a Space of Grace and Gratitude

Ilona Holland

In the bathroom, pregnancy test in hand, I placed my hand on my belly and smiled up at God, thanking Him for the precious gift He had placed in our care. Then I went into the next room to tell my husband, who was just as ecstatic about the news. In the coming weeks, the excitement grew as book recommendations from loving friends and family flooded our email inboxes. I read them voraciously, absorbing as much knowledge as I could, and felt empowered and overwhelmed in equal measure.

I made the most of this learning time, taking pages of notes. Every now and then a quote or sentence would tug at my strings (heart, mind, emotion… more… all). An article online sent me into a hysterical wave of tears (okay, okay, hormones were also at play here) and transported me back to various episodes during my childhood and teenage years. The words jostled my subconscious, tickled my thinking mind, and triggered all sorts of emotions about my ability to be a good mother. In a flash, anger, hate, bitterness, and revenge rippled through me. I cried and bit into my pillow, inhaling my husband's scent, a glimpse of consolation knowing I was not alone in this. I began to relive the lack of control I'd felt while growing up. The feeling of not being heard. I had taken it all; I never spoke back. Deep within me something had wanted to scream and yell, but it never happened.

Throughout these years I heard so many things about myself, so many labels based solely on the perceptions of others. And because they came from parents and teachers, principals, and priests, I accepted them without question. To my young ears they rang true, and why wouldn't they? After all, I am my father's daughter. I am my mother's too. I'm a sinner, and when I slipped up those on the receiving end of my behavior let me hear about it. To this day, parts of me still yearn for their forgiveness. I would re-live the humiliation and guilt over and over. I journeyed through life, absorbing and believing these words and allowing them to drown out my own inner voice. I often revolted, both against myself and against systems and individuals of higher authority; I hid behind my jokes and mockery of others, distancing myself from my authentic power and purity. The situation at home, at school, my first job... these were all psychologically challenging. In secondary school my actions and behavior seemed to support the labels placed upon me by others. Although I was, and am, grateful for all my parents provided me, I felt alone.

This aching solitude continued into my adult years. All the memories would play on a reel in my mind, even more vividly than when the event originally occurred. I "watched" as person after person turned their back on me—sometimes due to my own actions—and felt the loss and desperation as keenly as ever. Others laughed at my behavior, even when it was inappropriate and all about ridiculing others, all about passing on the psychological abuse. They didn't know it was my way of crying out: Someone help me! Some things in life were simply not up for discussion. What happens at home stays at home, and everywhere else, for that matter.

There would be many experiences that would drag me back through the same guilt and pain. Many situations in which it was the adults' responsibility to protect the vulnerability of such a young soul. Weren't the guardians, teachers, parents, grandparents and those whose care we were placed in supposed to have learned self-discipline? Shouldn't they have clear heads and hearts and an understanding and cultivation of their emotional maturity? In doing so, would their authentic selves shine true and thus notice my heart's deepest desires?

The answer to these questions is yes, of course they should; but the truth is, they often don't. Even as a child I knew I was not meant to see, hear, or be part of this dynamic. Years later, as I awaited the birth of my own child, I realized that earlier events had instilled in me several harmful belief systems that I had been carrying around ever since:

I am a liar; I am unworthy; I am scum; I am a hypocrite. I am not to be trusted, I deserve all the pain and suffering that comes to me. I am everything horrible my parents say about each other. I have let them both down. No one will want me to be better than them. I will never amount to anything.

It was through journaling that I finally began to unravel the twists and turns of my outer experiences and how they impacted my inner world. Like all of us, my life had its own cast of characters of varying importance. At center stage were my parents, grandparents, teachers, and friends with their own outer experiences filtering into their inner world, projected in this lifetime. They had shaped the script and thus the course and unfolding of this journey. There were days when the script moved from comedy to drama and suddenly back again.

As I rewrote and reviewed my journal entries, I began to notice two main scripts, interspersed with one another. I also saw the role that I played in them. For the first time I realized it was my choice. I saw myself identifying with the script that was fueled mainly by drama.

The other script was one of grace, gratitude, love, peace, and joy, and in that "play" the characters appeared as angels, sticking to God's calling and seeing more than met the eye. They looked past the jealousy and anger I was exhibiting and gave me the loving care I so desperately needed. As I read the second script I saw the truth of my life: angels are everywhere, in heaven and on earth. That angel is in everyone. God sends you angels in human form, "people of exemplary conduct and virtue." He certainly sent many to me along my journey.

My first was my father. He remains to this day, one of the very first signs from God that I am loved, I am light, and I am not alone. He was one of those characters, in my movie that moved from one script to another. While I did lash out and hurt him, his character would eventually be one of the best gifts to help me realize and recognize the light in myself and others. He would teach me the ease and error with which we place our expectations on others, only to have the castles we built come crashing down.

There were those characters that would follow their God-written part and see the light in me. Their love and care would bring me into their arms, offering me the safe space to talk, reflect, and breathe. Although I remember wanting to be held (a desire that went unfulfilled), I am forever grateful for the space my father and other individuals gave me to be and share. They asked the perfect questions that would bring me back to that strong voice which is, was, and always will be inside each of us. The voice that says: You are not alone. You are My unique child and I created you, therefore I will always love you and never leave your side. I give you the gifts of emotions, feelings, and virtues... Choose to use them to do My good work. Listen to Me in the depths of your heart and soul.

Some characters can bring you to the point of madness, but with God you will see that they too have something of greatness to pass on. They too have a purpose He's set in the depths of their hearts. Perhaps they too weren't listened to. I was in my early thirties before I realized that my mother (who drives me nuts) was my second most valuable teacher. Self-discipline echoed in the way she religiously made the bed, kept the home in immaculate condition, never made excuses, and always showed up. I learned from her our innate ability to self-regulate without needing someone to keep me in line.

Whatever the quality of my actions and words, these angels lifted me up, believed in me, and brought me back up to God, just where I had come from. They could have chosen to move along to someone who seemed more "promising," but they did not. Instead they saw in me the potential in all of us, despite our behavior or poor choices. They saw the potential in me, even when I did not see it in myself. To this day, some of these angels do not know how much of a gift they were and still are to me. All a gift from God.

What beliefs are you holding about yourself? Whatever they are, let me tell you right now—you are unique, you are light, you are not alone. God is presenting Himself in all living beings that cross our paths. If you take a moment to breathe ever so softly and calmly, rest in His arms and listen, you will hear Him. This is your eternal compass, the very heart of your being, the source of your true desires.

You've no doubt had your share of lessons, and there will be more to come. Take the lesson but let others' beliefs and projections bounce off of you, for they are just acting out their own "dramas." If you've absorbed or continue to carry these projections, it's time to release them. Perhaps journaling will give you a canvas on which to lay down your true voice and feelings, as it has done for me.

In my case, a variety of therapies, treatments, exercises, yoga, meditation, and self-care would also prove important. Some pivotal moments happened while in the safe space of the psychologist's office or during Thetahealing®. Whereas I used to hide behind food and alcohol, I now clung to a combination of practices that strengthened the Body, Mind, and Spirit. On those days I did not want to go on, I looked to my teachers/angels present in all of my experiences and chose to see the good in every being and situation. And in those moments, I learned the true meaning of grace. A grace I impart as a mother to my little boy of light and love and his sibling (on the way) with confidence. We are all on a journey doing the best we know how.

For everyone and everything, I am grateful.

ABOUT THE AUTHOR: Ilona Holland is a certified ThetaHealer®, Relaxation Therapist, Reiki Practitioner II, Life Coach and Yoga Instructor. Born with a passion for understanding the interrelation between Body, Mind, and Spirit, she has spent the past two decades traveling, studying, and practicing a variety of fitness and wellness techniques geared to helping fulfill people's holistic wellness goals. Today, she uses a combination of massage and other modalities to help children and adults understand what story the pain, tightness, or ailment in their body is trying to tell and facilitate the healing and balancing process. Ilona lives in Omaha, Nebraska with her husband and two-year-old son.

Ilona Holland
Life Dimensions by Ilona
ilonaholland.com
facebook.com/Life-Dimensions-by-Ilona-203965116343739
twitter.com/ilona_holland

Pearly Playgrounds
Kathleen Kraskouskas

I was raised in a Catholic household and in my adult life strayed from my religious upbringing. It would be a life-changing injury that both rekindled my relationship with God and resulted in a career change from the financial sector to the bodywork arena.

My ultimate recovery stemmed from cranial sacral therapy sessions. I was thoroughly ensconced into what I felt and how my body responded. With God at my side I continued to expand my abilities and senses to see and feel beyond what is present in human form. I have had the privilege of working with individuals whose injuries go beyond the human landscape. Maria is one of these people.

When Maria arrived for her first cranial sacral therapy session she did not say much, only that she had spent the past four decades—most of her life—trying to feel better, only to be disappointed. It seemed she could not express what she was truly looking for so without further communication we agreed we would just get down to work.

Nothing spectacular happened in that first session; however, Maria did book another appointment, saying she felt more relaxed than she could remember. In our second session things really changed—for both of us. It was then that I saw my first angel: the Archangel Michael.

I still remember it so clearly. His presence was immense and my initial reaction was fear; yet, in less than a millisecond the room filled with glowing warmth and a soft beaming light which let me know that everything was okay. As I looked at the Archangel Michael one of the first things I noticed was the massive size of the feathers on his wings. The multi-layered, billowy depths and curves of each feather were magical. A deep molten brown outlined each feather followed by a layer of gold, which in turn ebbed into fluffy white cotton.

It was then I realized Archangel Michael was a warrior. His voice was strong and melodious as he informed me we were entering a battle field and that he would be with us. He said we would be sheltered in his protection enabling us to conquer whatever lay ahead. I felt at peace and ready to move forward even though I had no idea what was coming.

As soon as we began, I started hearing voices. Initially I was uncertain where they were coming from; yet, as I paid more attention I realized they were coming from Maria's body which startled me. This was my first experience "hearing voices" and as I looked at Archangel Michael I knew what I was hearing was real and to not be afraid.

It was then that I had the courage to share with Maria about the voices I was hearing emanating from her body. Maria bluntly stated that she had been diagnosed with multiple personality disorder; then she fell silent without further elaboration. Maria was now in her fifties with a successful career; she was also happily married and a mother of two. To the outside observer, there was no indication that this woman had suffered with this condition since childhood.

There were so many voices that I could not keep track of them; yet, one did emerge as the leader. He called himself Red and I could tell there was a special bond between Red and Maria. Through images Red showed me Maria's difficult and traumatic childhood and the abuse she had endured.

Susan, one of the other voices stepped forward wanting to be heard. When I told Maria that Susan had a message for her, Maria stopped me in my tracks and with authority told me she had never assigned names to the voices, only emotions. Susan was known as "Malice"; there was also "Sadness", "Anger", "Irritability", and others. As for Red; well their relationship was unique; he was not an emotion; he was a go-between; Red was just Red.

The voices were still present at the onset of our third session; as was the Archangel Michael. Not only did the voices continue but I also perceived that there were doors, so many doors, inside Maria.

The only way I could get my point across was to tell her it was like a morgue—but instead of drawers there were doors. As each door opened the emotions inside let us know they were there—and that they felt trapped. They wanted out.

It was then that Maria shed light on some of her counseling sessions from many years ago. Her therapist had asked her to create a safe haven for the voices. She remembered trying to encourage them to live in a lovely park; however, they sought refuge inside her body. After all these years she could still hear their voices.

It was at this point in our session the emotions kept pointing towards a "genie bottle" with currents of wind whipping around. No emotion would go close to the bottle for it contained the most horrific emotions Maria felt. Only God could touch it.

This was the first time Maria and I spoke about God. I told her Red said only God could handle the genie bottle. Would it be okay if we asked God to take it away? Without hesitation she gave permission.

Within seconds, a whirlwind of energy started swirling and a powerful hand swooped down and grabbed the genie bottle. I knew immediately it was the hand of God. Peace settled over Maria and the emotions. The rest of the session was completed in silence as we both took in how the emotions in the landscape of Maria's body had changed.

The removal of the bottle was so powerful it unlocked a door deep inside Maria. She was now strong enough to deal with all the voices. We talked about how she wanted them to be in a beautiful park, having fun and enjoying their lives; not in her body.

Each session brought more conversations about the emotions with God. We knew God had to be present when dealing with the remaining voices. After many years questioning her faith, Maria chose to humble herself and trust God to handle the voices.

What happened next can only be considered a gift. Before our eyes a golden staircase came down from heaven. At the top of the staircase was God and Red was at the bottom. God then gestured with His arms for all the voices to come to Him.

Some emotions went straight to the staircase, others danced

around celebrating; and others held back questioning what they should do. Red was instrumental in letting the emotions know they could trust God, the being at the top of the staircase. What was most important was that each of the emotions had to make its own decision to climb the stairs. While Maria let go; the voices had to trust her as well.

One by one they began to ascend the golden staircase. God welcomed each one and directed them to follow the "Path of Clouds." The voices were so joyful, they were light in foot; embracing and knowing they were on the way to somewhere fantastic. It was as if they were floating on air.

While Maria was happy to see this; sadness overcame her. The emotions were leaving her body. Her own feelings heightened and I could sense her feeling of loss. In a way these were her friends and even though she wanted them to leave; the feelings of loneliness and emptiness were becoming all too real.

After the last emotion climbed the staircase, Red made it clear that he was not leaving at this time. Red informed me he had to stay behind as he and Maria still needed to spend time with each other. Maria immediately agreed. The bond between Red and Maria was unique and lifesaving. Red made it possible for Maria to live her life, have a career and be a mother.

Maria, Red, and I continued to watch the emotions as they made their way down the Path of Clouds. As they neared the end of the path we could faintly make out what appeared to be gates. As the path ended and the clouds parted, we saw glistening, golden posts as far as the eye could see. Cherubic angels danced and laughed welcoming everyone to "The Pearly Playgrounds."

This was the beautiful, glorious park Maria had always envisioned. We were allowed to see into the gates of the Pearly Playground and see the beauty God had created for them. We were shown how fabulous their lives were while they waited for Maria to pick them up on her way to heaven. It was a glorious time.

Red and Maria spent three days together before he too ascended the golden staircase. Red had done a tremendous job managing all of these emotions. Maria humbly thanked Red and released him knowing they would meet again.

Following their ascent up the golden staircase and their arrival in the Pearly Playgrounds, Maria announced the voices were gone. For the first time her body was silent. We cried together as we both felt God's presence and realized how blessed we were to bear witness to these events.

The Archangel Michael played a critical role while these sessions took place. He kept vigilant in our unique surroundings so we could interact with the emotions, with Red and God. He established a perimeter we never had to question; allowing us to experience the wholeness of what was presented without regards to time and space.

Maria's life changed following these sessions, as did mine. We continued to talk about God and we both realized how merciful God is. We talked about how many people get angry with God when bad things happen and about how misplaced this anger is.

God does not create bad things in our lives, nor does He endorse them when they occur. It is when bad things happen that God shows us His mercy by carrying us, listening to us, loving us and bringing us closer to Him. After this experience Maria and I agreed that it is truly when one humbles oneself and gives the issue to God that true healing takes place.

Maria has gone on to retire, see her children marry and to continue with her international travels. She often comments on how enjoyable it is to just read a book, watch a movie, converse, and have quiet time all without a constant backdrop of voices. Peace is now hers, and she is eternally grateful for the unique gift God bestowed upon her.

I continue to pray and meditate on my conversations between God and myself. These practices allow for new insights and understandings. I have been told many times "You are a healer, an angel, etcetera." While I am moved by these statements, I cannot agree; for while my training introduced me to aspects of healing; it is, God's guidance that allowed for greater capacity to heal on levels we may not understand.

My relationship with God continues to deepen and flower. I feel grateful and privileged to interact with Him every day. Developing a relationship with God is the same as starting a relationship with any person. You must spend time with Him and nurture your relationship for it to be meaningful and real. I wish for you the same in your discovery of God.

ABOUT THE AUTHOR: Kathleen Kraskouskas is the owner of the Cranial Sacral Therapy Center in San Jose, California, where she employs cranial sacral therapy, neurofeedback, frequency/light therapy, and energy/intuitive medicine to affect healing. She was drawn to cranial sacral therapy after suffering a severe injury in her late twenties. The profound results led to an understanding of how the body repairs itself and inspired her to leave her career in finance and study cranial sacral therapy. Kathleen especially loves working with autistic children and is a founder of Angels Soaring, a charity dedicated to **A**utistic **N**eighbors **G**athering for **E**ducation and **L**iving **S**ustainably.

Kathleen Kraskouskas
Cranial Sacral Therapy Center
cranialsacraltherapycenter.com
cstkathleen@gmail.com
408-279-1122

You are the Gift
Klara Goldy

What is a Goddess?

A woman who is in the process of learning to know, accept, and love herself on all levels—Mind, Body, and Spirit.

A woman who, because she focuses on personal growth and self-awareness, experiences a life increasingly filled with peace, love, joy, passion, and fun.

A woman who understands she has unlimited capacity to make her life anything she wants.

A woman who is inspired to give to those around her, because of her sense of gratitude and abundance.

~ Unknown

Phew!!! Oh Lord, what a relief! I thought, as I leaned back on the other side of the front door I had just closed and found myself in the quiet and stillness, alone at home. The boys had just started at their new school and I had the house to myself. Suddenly, a sense of peace came over me; pausing to look around me, I still wondered if I had done the right thing, walking away from a marriage while I had two young sons. In this new independent life, there were days when I was shaky from a combination of excitement and trepidation at what I was creating!

So many events and experiences had gotten me to this point. My ex and I had simply stopped making each other happy. It wasn't because he wasn't a good man; he just did not have the capacity to meet me with spiritual depth or to be fully present. Our wants and needs were different.

In the beginning, we had come hurtling together as SOULS. It was a funny paradox, really, as we both had brought a ton of emotional baggage to our marriage. This baggage was acquired along the journey of life, and some of it was not even our own. It was just life, people, and the way that it gets projected out onto others. Lately, life had seemed to be a damage limitation exercise. After a stream of difficult and toxic relationships with people intent on being destructive or not able to see the joy in life, I was a nervous, emotional wreck in my marriage. Soon, it became an increasingly tough gig to be around all those flying emotions, all so charged; every piece flying around hurt, so I built up mechanisms to cope. But merely coping was clearly not a good long-term strategy.

Around the age of twenty-three, I had experienced severe panic attacks. Although I had long since recovered from this, it felt that I had overcome one set of problems only to exchange them for a new set. My inability to express my needs and to be heard didn't help either. Summoning the courage to walk away was nothing short of a miracle; starting over was a challenge in itself, and yet I was strong deep down, very strong. (Later, I learned just how deep my strength went).

When I finally left my marriage, I thought, *this is a chance to become the woman I know I was born to be, a time for a new way of being.* I gave myself full permission to acknowledge that, and to even savor the thought of becoming whole. My body sighed in deep relief at that thought. Would I be able to access and trust my intuition? Recently, I had caught myself overriding my intuition: this whispered voice or inner knowing would tell me something about how to proceed in the moment, and then I would ignore it, only to find that the inner guidance was right! Here came the challenge of how to empower myself and honor this internal process. Would I be able to teach myself a way that was more congruent with my heart? These were the questions I needed answers to, but who was I asking them to? I was asking a lot of questions to myself in those days. I had to learn to love the different aspects of myself and discover what it is to be an authentically powerful woman.

I did not want to be defined by others' perceptions or have the views of others imposed upon me or decided for me by society's definition of what a woman *should* be. No, this was a time for reinvention. Cultural influences had engineered a belief of what it was to be a woman based on manipulation through religious and political channels. So here I was: repressed creatively and unable to express my feelings, yet my courage was burning bright.

There was a new sense of urgency and optimism within me. I knew that if I were to come to grips with my life and my emotions, if I could master my feminine essence, and if I could learn to be congruent with my heart, I was going to be successful in my life. Later, I would learn that I was a sensitive empath and soul connector, a seer who can read the energy world and cross over realms. My strong inner guidance was there from a very young age, just this beautiful stillness and grace, guiding me and talking to me. Nobody told me much about this stuff, only my father, who had mentioned that my late grandmother of Irish descent was a psychic. Although he didn't speak much about it, my father was quietly proud of this fact, and it made me wonder about where that ability came from.

Now that I was alone in the house, the stillness came over me again; it was as if I were being breathed through. I walked into the sitting room. It was looking good these days, as I had worked hard to recreate the space into a warm, light, calm family room. I had opened up the fireplace so that we could light a fire in the winter months. I love the sense of connecting to the elements and hearing the crackle and spittle of logs burning and glowing. There is a deeply shamanic practice in fire building and fire tending; it is as if when you watch the flames dance and pirouette, they can burn away past hurts and wounds. By this point, my whole life was built on deeply sensing things around me. Living in this fully present way makes life interesting. Grateful for this deep guidance; I had learned techniques to help protect myself from some of the more challenging experiences.

I sat down on the soft sofa and gazed gently into the center of the room, half closing my eyes... letting myself drift. More and more these days, I was starting to let myself off the hook from the invasive driven work ethic mentality, which could rob me of joy. This half-state of relaxation and dreaming was me giving myself permission to allow something else more beautiful to flood in, to allow for some new energy to arrive and set me free from the drive for survival. I was in the mode of deepening into this guidance.

This time was used to reflect on the external support that had helped me to gain so much more clarity around the journey of living and being, allowing an awakening of my emotions and senses. This was my way to celebrate the beauty in life even in the simple things—a flower shimmering in the sun, the way the birds dance and pirouette in midair, the smiles and laughter of my boys.

Rousing myself gently, I went over to the cupboard where I kept a box of incense. This cupboard was a place for keeping my meditation supplies and sacred items. Inside the cupboard, there were my box of crystals (rose quartz for love, amethyst for creativity) some pretty tea light candles, and a box of angel cards. I found the inspirational words on the cards comforting and uplifting. Here it was: a small, round, painted tray—a junkshop find. I ran my fingers over the Italianate edging, the faded pink and blue antiqued patterns, and its golden rim.

Celebration of the little things and gratitude for the beauty was part of setting intention in the house. My sitting room was the main place I consecrated to be a sacred area, and the little tray served as the altar. At this altar, I practiced meditation on all the things I was grateful for and I made a small prayer to ask for divine inspiration to flow through me. As an awakening healer, I asked that I might be a vehicle for love and light in my own life.

Each day as I meditated, I allowed myself permission to feel what I needed to feel in order to help me set up my day in a way that felt calm and loving, to help me to deal with life situations that were thrown at me, and to be able to deal with difficult people with power, kindness, and ease. I prayed that I would find a way to be true to myself and not make another feel hurt by expressing my truth.

I looked forward to this time of meditation, to sliding into that World, lying still, to connecting with my breathing. Playing sacred chants or ethereal music enhanced this state. It helped me to create my life as an act of service. To experience the extraordinary through celebration sustained me at core level; it reminded me of all the good things that I had to be grateful for. It was tapping me into a higher resonance of positivity and literally preventing my brain from thinking the opposite. I needed my sacred sessions to experience those feelings of beauty through dream states, closing out all the noise of any aggression and anger, closing out a world that had seemed to have forgotten sacred beauty.

I struck the match and lit the incense: as I placed it on the pretty tray it caused me to reflect how by deepening into the act of celebration gives us an access point, a powerful and important way of making our realities into the ones we dream about. It's the one hundred little things we do, the small tokens and gestures of kindness that make connections and friendships and create warmth. Putting our focus on that which we want to see and create in our lives causes these things to expand. Such is the power of the heart.

I had been learning from a wise soul who was teaching me how the components of our inner Worlds are what we are connected to; this invisible component is a connection to the energy realm or quantum field, where everything is blueprinted from outside of time and space. Everything here is connected and unified.

Setting up these meditation and sacred sessions allowed me to understand that the state of energy and spirit is not measurable through the rational mind. We have to, in part, surrender the mind to some greater part of us. It is truly the Spirit World where the power comes from and when we get comfortable with this in a physical sense, we can feel it and sense it. It is a natural as breathing, once we tap into it. Rituals allow us to maintain a state of communion, and connection to our inner world allows us to flow effortlessly, realizing that the stream of consciousness is the river and once you allow it to enter your life as this divine communion, you can go into its flow.

The trick is to get the mind out of the way. The mind can become a dangerous master if we are not careful, sabotaging us and robbing us of our joy by the tricks it plays. We are here to remember what we truly are. During the time of my commitment to daily meditation, I was learning to find this more and more in the breath, in the pause right between the inhale and exhale. Our individual self and soul is the bridge to Spirit. The beauty of the ceremony and ritual we set up teaches us how to connect to that field of the heart where expansion can take place.

So many times, my soul slides easily into other worlds, including what I call the Sacred Dream World. There, I am sometimes passing over with dying friends or relatives, sometimes recognizing the sound of a voice from a past life or a SOUL family member. This sliding over can happen simply in the connection to the beauty of nature or to the sunset in its dizzying, melting heat of tantric ripples. Each time we connect to the HEART, we experience that which is sublime and powerful beyond measure, and we enter into the state of GRACE and deep eternal LOVE.

How my life has changed since those early days when my marriage first dissolved! I am so grateful that my bigger, beautiful soul continues to breathe through me, expanding my consciousness. It is the bridge to Spirit, which is my abiding truth and the way the divine feminine has brought such sweetness to my life. It has truly been a gift, the gift of my whole self.

ABOUT THE AUTHOR: Klara Goldy is an author, creative leader, empowerment coach, and owner of Divine by Design. Klara's work guides you to enhance yourself from the inside out by aligning your inner essence with your unique soul blueprint. Using the spiritual psychology of colour, chakra wisdom, soul alignment and shamanic energy principle in gratitude she was led to create the "Diamond Alignment Program" a system to help understand your divine emotional intelligence. Klara assists you to master your Soul Gifts for Success.

Klara Goldy ~ Divine by Design
Life from the inside out
+44 242 3221472
klaragoldy.com
vcita.com/v/klaragoldy

Cosmic 2x4
Mija Cameto

I woke up to my left leg numb and tingling. I was 21 years old, and it was finals week of Winter Quarter 1995 at University of California, San Diego. I was also in physical therapy for multiple back injuries and fractures throughout my teen years that had resulted in chronic pain and eventually some dysfunction. At my PT appointment later that same day I mentioned to my therapists that both of my legs had been numb a couple of years before. "Maybe it will go away," we wondered. The next morning, both legs were numb and tingling, and the following morning, I was numb from the chest down! The student health physician referred me to a neurologist, who immediately got me in for blood work and MRIs. I was inside the MRI tube for over an hour, mostly numb, for who knows what reason, and I vividly remember enjoying the power of "simple pleasures" as I listened with nostalgia to Jim Croce through the headphones.

A day later I was sitting in the neurologist's office, and while he said the words "Multiple Sclerosis" I had the sensation and visual experience of looking through two eye holes, then almost like sliding to the left and looking out through two new eye holes. My life perception viscerally and completely changed in that moment. I didn't actually know what it meant, but I knew it was one of the "big diseases."

I read everything I could get my hands on, which in the days before the internet was widely accessible, was found mostly in textbooks and pamphlets. It *was* big. Anything in the brain or spinal cord could be affected. My own immune system was attacking the myelin, the protein sheaths around nerves that allow them to conduct electricity, like the plastic around wires. Common symptoms were visual disturbances, numbness, dizziness, organ dysfunction, cognitive issues, and eventually in some cases paralysis, organ failure, and death.

Most of me was shocked and scared beyond belief. Part of me was relieved, because I finally had answers to why I had numb, tingling legs two years before. A year before that was dizziness that kept me on the couch a few weeks. And two years before that was numbness and tingling from the knees down for a few weeks. Now I had answers to the mysteries.

The brightest aspect of that first week was the incredible support I received from my friends, even while they were dealing with their own finals. Over spring break I went back to my hometown in Northern California to get a second opinion, including a lumbar puncture or spinal tap. I stayed perfectly horizontal on the couch or in bed for twenty-four hours, even while eating, to avoid the dreaded "spinal tap headache."

I was signed up for a support program for the "newly diagnosed." Everyone I spoke to had such varied symptoms, but some were similar to mine. Connecting with other people was helpful, but also surreal, and at times disturbing as their symptoms were sometimes far worse. Was this my future?

My symptoms progressed after the initial diagnosis. My legs felt like wide, tight bands were sometimes constricting just above my knees, a form of spasticity. One day I tried to sit at a cafe table and my legs wouldn't go under. When I looked under the table, I could see they were against the table leg. I couldn't feel the pressure, but a pin prick test in the neurologist's office had felt twenty times sharper. When anything cold, even a wind, touched my legs, especially the left one, it felt like a cross between electric shock and acid burn. When I took a shower, I had to first run a warm bath, slowly immerse myself, then turn on and stand up into the shower. Stepping into the water droplets was excruciatingly impossible. I was probably the only person in San Diego wearing thermal underwear. I had learned in physiology class there are different nerve endings for sensation, pressure, and temperature, but now I knew exactly how separate they were.

I could no longer hold my bladder like a normal twenty-something-year-old. At some point my cognitive function declined.

I would be mid-sentence or mid-paragraph and suddenly have no idea what I was talking about. It felt shocking and embarrassing, so sometimes I felt like crying, sometimes I just got quiet, then would apologize and attempt to explain. Instead of occasionally forgetting a word, it was happening regularly.

One of the hardest aspects was the heat sensitivity. I could not allow my internal temperature or heart rate to go up, or I lost overall function. I woke up once in a sun saturated guest room at my college boyfriend's parents' home. He found me barely responsive. Luckily he knew to open the window and cover me with cool, wet washcloths. I carried a brick sized cell phone for emergency calls only, because the idea of my car breaking down in the sun was terrifying. One day I started walking up the street from my house, but after about a block, my legs felt like they each weighed five hundred pounds. I had to stop and sit.

One strange symptom was that everything intensified when I would bend my neck, putting my chin on my chest, or if I would push my upper body up when laying on my stomach. My spinal cord was very sensitive within my own spinal column.

Over the next months some symptoms got better, but the heat sensitivity lasted for about four years. I couldn't let my internal temperature increase, and it seemed most everything in my life was decided around this. Every time I moved, the new apartment or house had to have a bath tub. The spine positioning of bending my neck or low back created symptoms for years, even when mostly gone.

I moved back to Northern California in 1998, and in 2002 my new neurologist said he'd like to get a follow-up MRI and put me on the latest greatest medication that could prevent me from getting any worse. Self-injecting into muscle, I went from no problems with needles to panic attacks. The interferon medication also had the side effect of overwhelming suicidal ideation. I had moments where I felt so deep, dark and horrific all I wanted was to explode into a million pieces and disappear completely. I was put on an anti-depressant to counteract this side effect, which worked at first, but after a few months it started to lose effect. I decided I would not play the "up the dose, then try a new anti-depressant" game I had heard about, and self-weaned the interferon and then the anti-depressant.

During one of the deep, dark times, I called out from somewhere within me, "HELP!!" Shortly after that I was reading a book, and in the final pages the name of a survival training camp caught my eye. On their website, a description about one of the teachers listed the term "Reiki Master." I didn't know what it meant, and I felt an overwhelming need to find out. The first search link I clicked on said "...excellent for multiple sclerosis..." I was stunned. I found a local practitioner who referred me to his teacher. I asked her to explain it to me, and she said it was better for me to just experience it for myself. My usually scientific mind surrendered immediately, and I booked an appointment.

With my first session I felt an uncanny sense of "greater well-being." I was hooked, and went for a Reiki treatment every week. Soon I could feel energy moving through my body, like water, or warmth, or sparkles. My neurologist eventually called me into his office. "I'm kicking you out. You're the healthiest person in my practice. Keep doing what you're doing." He looked at his notes on his clipboard, shaking his head, saying under his breath, "There's something about attitude!" I smiled, thanked him, and left.

In 2006 my best friend handed me a little book called *Heal Your Body: The Mental Causes for Physical Illness and the Metaphysical Way to Overcome Them*. I looked up MS, read the probable cause, and thought "this doesn't describe me" and left it on the counter. "They don't know what they're talking about. None of my friends would call me hard-hearted!"

Over the next year, I had three separate situations where I had an internal response, an emotional defensiveness, that I would have called "steeling myself." There were also three exacerbations of MS symptoms, although I did not see the correlation at first. During the first onset of MS symptoms, I called my neurologist who asked if my symptoms were old ones or new ones. When I responded with "old ones," he said "Let me know if they are new, we will admit you to the hospital and start prednisone." I had been on that drug before for a blood disorder, and while very helpful, I thoroughly knew its unwanted potential side effects. I acknowledged his plan, hung up, and laid on the couch. In the past I had found great emotional stress relief through meditation; twenty minutes of visualizing myself as a human-sized plate of dried rice, that I slowly dislodged grain by grain until I could scoop and sweep my "plate self" clean. Another time I was a tarnished bronze statue that I rubbed until it sparkled and gleamed. This time I spontaneously imagined myself as a light bulb, filled myself with white light, then radiated and expanded until I became the light and fell asleep. I woke up a bit later, went on with life, and within a day or two I felt fine.

After the second symptom onset, I finally recognized the similar internal "frequency" of steeling myself and the time delay of the physical MS symptoms. The book had said, "Mental hardness, hardheartedness, iron will, inflexibility. Fear." I caught myself much sooner through the third situation, let it go, and the MS symptoms were fleeting.

If I catch myself "down the MS path" I have learned to think of it as my "cosmic 2x4." Choose a higher road, now, or else! I've been repeatedly "forced" into what has become an incredible spiritual journey, and one of the greatest gifts of my life. If I let the emotional defensiveness go a little too long, I feel like my nerves are about to catch fire, and I simply can no longer take another step down that path. I stop, let go, and lay down. I meditate on my breath, exhaling completely, releasing everything... physical tension, mental stressors, emotional anxieties. I imagine myself like a light bulb, filled with and radiating pure white light, then expand and become the light, until I am no longer "me", no longer a gender, race, or a story of any kind, until I am simply allowing and receiving unconditional love and unlimited wellness. I know and trust from many years of practice that I will be right as rain within twenty-four to forty-eight hours, and the most symptoms I have felt is a prickle on my upper back that tells me, "Good job! Close call."

I have received such grace on this journey, some of which I allowed for myself in the form of self-love and the determination and openness to try new ways to health. There have also been countless blessings from others—from college friends who found time during their own studies to support me during the diagnosis, to the neurologist who released me when he saw what I was doing was working, to my best friend who gave me the book on how to heal through changes in perception. I am overwhelmed with gratitude for every person and situation I have encountered along the way, for each has empowered me to move forward in wholeness, self-discovery and wonder.

ABOUT THE AUTHOR: Mija Cameto was raised fourth generation immersed in western surgical medicine, with innate talents for and deeply passionate about the human body since childhood through science, mathematics, anatomy, physiology, artistic expression, movement, bodywork, meditation, and consciousness. After decades of personal illnesses, conditions, and injuries in every system and location of her body, her teaching and consulting work are the culmination of living a synchronistic and guided path further into wellness than she could have ever imagined. It is an honor and a gift to assist others to find their own path.

Mija Cameto, CMT #68843
Therapeutic & Relaxation Massage
Mind Body Wellness Consultant
MijaCameto.com
916-769-9813

Breathe In Faith
Rev. Anita Nicole Mas

This morning I woke to the sound of waves crashing on the shore and a soft, warm breeze washing over my body. Waking *every* morning in my penthouse apartment along the coast of Caribbean Sea always feels like some delicious dream. As I walk out of my bedroom and am greeted by the panoramic view of the coast I take a deep breath in and give thanks to the Divine for allowing me to see my Heart's Desire manifest in such vibrant, vivid color.

It was not long ago that I was a struggling, single mother living on the welfare system. My life had taken a nose dive, and truthfully, it wasn't hard to see why. It started when I left my home and a successful energy practice in Toronto and moved with my daughter's father to a new city. Although I did not want to leave my life behind, I wanted to be supportive, and he promised his new job would bring us security. Yet, even as I prepared to move, I felt something was off. He was acting differently, but whenever I questioned him, he swore it was just work stress. I tried to ignore my feelings, until one night I came face to face with them…literally.

One evening after dinner I opened the computer and there was his Facebook account, opened up to the romantic messages he'd shared with his lover. I stared in shock and disbelief. It was as if my entire system was placed on pause. For three days, I couldn't think or feel a thing. I walked around in a daze. I went from being an active, engaged mother who played with her two- year-old and focused on living a healthy life to not having the energy to eat or focus on much at all. It felt as though all the life had left my body.

For seven months I waded through the mash of emotions— everything from hating and blaming him to agreeing to go to couples therapy and working it out. My moods cycled on a daily and sometimes hourly basis—from disgust, sadness and anger to forgiveness and desperation. Sometimes I even begged him to make it work. Finally, I moved back to Toronto, realizing that I was unable to forgive him and he was not ready to be forgiven. Still he was full of promises, telling me he was going to heal, change, and come back to me and Lyla a changed man. He just needed to be alone, he said, time to "figure out his shit." About nine months later he finally admitted that he was in another relationship, and had been since the time I left. We were over. Still I could not let this go and spent yet another six months playing out this illusion. I even continued to sleep with him. I didn't see this as cheating on his current girlfriend, because I still saw him as mine.

All this time I felt like I was stuck in quicksand. I was not attracting clients, which wasn't surprising considering my state of mind, I had to apply for welfare as he rarely paid child support and when he did it was very little. I could not get a regular job because whatever I made would have gone to a nanny to look after my daughter. Nothing made sense and I felt like I couldn't hold my head above water for much longer.

The turning point came that New Year's Eve. After putting Lyla, now four years old, down for the night, I sat there and calmly reviewed my life, owning my drama and my illusions, and forcing myself to confront the truth. I had always known we would never marry. Months before I saw the Facebook page, I'd had dreams of him cheating. Even during my pregnancy I felt the truth: this was not the man I would be spending my life with. I'd buried those thoughts by convincing myself it was me and my own negative thinking. Now, I used the energy techniques I had been teaching for years to move through this pain, see my truth and decide once and for all to let this man go.

Immediately, I began to attract clients again. I focused on manifesting an abundant life. I began to manifest Yoga as a career and to "be my life." Out of nowhere, a friend of mine from whom I had rented space for my healing work offered to partner with me in opening a Yoga studio!

Our agreement was pretty simple—I would run the studio and she would finance it. I knew the first year of any business was the hardest. My partner offered to pay me $500 a month until the business could afford to pay me—an offer I gratefully accepted. In the meantime, I would continue to use welfare to make ends meet. Then, a month after the studio opened she told me she was also in financial trouble and could no longer pay me. So, there I was... working a minimum of 12 hours a day, taking care of my daughter who had just started half-days in kindergarten, making no money from my work and still collecting welfare.

Desperate to make the studio work, I started living off a credit card, both to supplement my personal expenses and shortages at the studio. In short, I was making a huge mistake! I saw this studio coming into my life as "meant to be" since I had been manifesting it. I was desperate for a life where I didn't have to worry about money, didn't care whether or not Lyla's father was paying child support; I thought Yoga was the answer. I thought if I just keep moving forward soon it would all turn out. I had to try harder and not give up! Six months later, however, my body gave up. Bronchitis visited me and I could not leave my bed for a week. Alone and with no support system close by, I continued to care for my daughter while sick and run the studio from my bed. This illness showed me I was putting too much energy into the business. I decided to take a vacation to clear my head and my energy, and I had just enough left on my credit card to make this happen. We went to Mexico, where my heart had been longing to go for twenty years, and that's when everything changed.

Spending this time in Mexico—unplugged—helped me to see that the studio was draining me. Then another thought entered my mind, and took hold: I saw how easy it could be to *move* to Mexico! It was much less expensive, which meant I could be finished with welfare. I felt a deep pull inside of me and knew I had to make it happen, yet I still didn't want to give up the studio that I had just poured my heart and soul into. I knew it would start making money soon and wanted to be part of that. One day I had a vision of me, asking a teacher I trusted to manage the place. It seemed like a perfect solution. However, unbeknownst to me, there was another energy at play. There was a woman back in Toronto who I had taken in under my wing; I gave her a free space to work, classes in exchange for some work she did around the studio, and tried to help her in any other way I could. As I would soon find out, she was actually a wolf in sheep's clothing. She spread rumors that I was stealing money from my own business and that I was cheating my partner, who, not surprisingly, became angry with me. The energy around the studio I loved had become dense and uncomfortable.

When the teacher I'd asked to manage suddenly quit without explanation, I began to think I would have to close the studio. Then, two weeks before I was about to leave for Mexico, another woman appeared who was perfect for the job. We signed the contract and off I went thinking everything was great. By the end of the following month everything had fallen apart. People were accusing me of ripping my partner off, and the "perfect" manager had cleared out my bank account. I couldn't pay the rent! Since I didn't have the money to fly back and deal with it in person, I was forced to close the studio. A few days later I learned that two teachers who had worked with me had now, along with my ex-partner, taken it over. I was devastated that people I trusted had believed the lie and turned their backs on me. Yet, underneath the hurt was a louder voice inside me. This voice knew that even though this looked so dark and hurtful, Spirit had another plan for me. I felt grateful that my vision of these teachers was in fact coming true and the studio would continue. I knew I was in the right place even though it looked completely different from the outside. I forgave everyone involved as I understood they did not know the truth and acted from what they thought they knew.

From this moment on I began focusing on being grateful for being in a place that was so beautiful and healing for me. I could spend time with my daughter, who I had missed terribly while working so much. At the same time I had to figure out how I was going to survive in Mexico. As I focused on giving thanks every morning and every evening, clients and students began to contact me. As I connected with myself daily, I felt a deep sense that there was a higher purpose to me being in Mexico. I was to meet someone here...

One morning I opened my door and there he was. My heart stopped and jumped into my throat. I stepped back inside and slammed the door. That was him! I just knew it. Within weeks, we knew we would be together; all we had to do was figure out the logistics.

Today I can hardly believe the beautiful life we have manifested right here on the coast of the Caribbean Sea. We treat each other with respect and dignity. He loves my daughter and treats her as his own. We also share a Yoga and Energy Work business, where we help people heal; I also travel to teach. Every day we look into each other's eyes and say, "Thank you for being here." We use energy techniques to keep our energy clear and to solve issues that arise between us. We live in this moment and offer deep gratitude that by the Grace of Divine we found each other and have this life together. I see how all this turmoil had to be part of my life, yet I also understand that I could have let go of the drama sooner if I'd only trusted that more was waiting for me. Now, I'm teaching these powerful techniques to others so they may too realize that there is a higher plan for us, a plan that naturally falls into place when we can see the blessings we have been given, align ourselves with Divine Will, and follow our Hearts. I am living proof!

ABOUT THE AUTHOR: Nicole Mas has been teaching Spiritual and Energy concepts since 2006. After studying Spiritual Psycho-therapy she became a Reiki and Integrated Energy Therapy Master-Instructor and an Ordained Metaphysical Reverend. As a spiritual guide she teaches, supports and empowers individuals and groups in finding their Divine purpose, clearing blocks that hold them back, and manifesting the life of their dreams. It is Nicole's Joy to teach these energetic techniques that have greatly supported her in her own personal life. Currently, she is working closely with the Angelic Realm to support humanity in understanding and moving through the Ascension and also writing her first book.

Rev. Anita Nicole Mas
The Healing Experience
Journey Into Self & Back to Spirit
NicoleMas.com
info@nicolemas.com

The Gift of
Rose-Colored Glasses
Beatriz Schriber

My life—the only one I can speak of with any sort of authority—has been full of both challenges and gifts. I can honestly say that Grace (which I firmly believe is available to everyone) has invariably shown up, meeting me at every turn, oftentimes without me realizing it. She has appeared in countless forms and shapes. She has had many names and faces. When I look back, I recognize her as the source of my inner strength, empowering me from within or reaching to me from outside myself, always inviting me to bounce back, to keep going. Little by little, I learn to recognize her on the spot. Our encounters have been teaching me to trust, and as I jot down these grace-full encounters in a gratitude journal, my "trust muscle," once again torn only enough to build, builds. How can I not trust in God, in Life, in a Universe that is inherently benevolent, even if at times it doesn't appear to be? And yet, sometimes I forget. I start resisting life and feel the contraction and constriction inside. Even then, Grace steps in once more and provides me with what I need to open my eyes, my mind, and my heart to once again, let life in.

Several years ago, I was faced with the challenge of caring for my husband who, after an unfortunate accident, followed by what in his case turned out to be devastating effects from anesthesia, was never able to return home. The aftermath of this shocking turn of events has been dramatic. During his almost three months at a rehab facility, it was required that someone be with him at all times to keep him from getting out of bed or out of his wheelchair and falling. One of my daughters and I took turns and were intermittently supported by a handful of friends and some family. In spite of the close supervision, we still had to make several trips to the hospital. He was eventually transferred to a memory care facility. There, in further shifted circumstances, the challenges remained while our support system slowly faded from the scene. Wanting to lovingly support him and being his primary bridge to the world he used to know, I devotedly went to see him practically every day. Contrary to medical expectations, his condition kept improving. He got himself to walk, played Bingo to win me chocolates, and laughed with those sparkling, blue eyes, until an antibiotic-resistant bacteria finally took its toll three years later. This chapter of my life, where Grace was so present, merits the writing of a book.

It was one day during those challenging times that I had the opportunity to briefly chat with a well-renowned researcher in the fascinating field of neuroscience. Burdened and exhausted, I timidly yet boldly asked him: "Knowing all that you know, what does one do when everything looks dark and life seems hopeless?" I was expecting an elaborate and technical response, so his simple answer surprised me: "Well, you put on your rose-colored glasses." It couldn't be any simpler! I recall him having said that the brain's main assignment is our survival, so it has to constantly scan for, detect, guard against, and find ways of dealing with any perceived threat. As it conspires to find the negative, it takes an act of will to see, instead, the positive.

So what does that mean? And where does one find those "magic" glasses? Are we to fool ourselves pretending that the threat is not there? Do we follow the "ostrich approach?" Do we try to find that "elusive fine line" between what's in front of our eyes and what we want to see? Do we just wish the black pink? And where is the heart in all of this? And the body? And the soul? Can they all be aligned and reconciled? I had so many questions! And then, intuitively, I knew that what I was looking for had to be my very own answer.

I have come to realize that those magic glasses are within; that we carry them with us all the time. That it's not about pretending, switching, or even superimposing. It's more about making a pause, taking a breath, noticing the feelings in our heart as well as where they are felt in our body, and consciously looking within through those rose-colored glasses to find the inner compass that connects us to joy and thus to life, eventually leading us to inner peace. It's about seeing and appreciating with our whole being the gift of any experience.

It's about being present, connecting to our body—that awesome vehicle that we have been graciously given to dwell in and that houses our being while in this world. To move, to feel alive as we fill our lungs with air and sense our heart pumping and our blood flowing with the rhythm of life! We all need to find our own way. For me, the most meaningful one, ever since I can remember, has been dancing. I have been exposed to countless forms and enjoyed almost all of them. Then, many years ago, I was introduced to PanEuRhythmy, a beautiful dance meditation from Bulgaria, which is one of the most precious gifts I have received in this lifetime.

It was love "at first sight"—I only needed to hear the first three notes of the music to feel that I had to have it in my life. My soul was touched, and the love affair continues to this day. The principles behind it, the beauty of the music, the simplicity of the movements, the depth of their meaning, the power and poetry of the words, the sense of Oneness, as well as the benefits at all levels of our being, are impossible to describe—I consider it instrumental in my healing of breast cancer almost seventeen years ago. Danced outdoors, it is a profound and nurturing experience that is to be fully lived as a sacred and healing, joyful exchange between Man-Nature-Source. In the words of the Master Peter Deunov, who created it in the 1900's, "PanEurhythmy is the key which will bring Peace to the human soul… and people will grasp the meaning of their lives." It has certainly helped me! And part of my contribution in life is to share this gentle yet powerful teaching as much as I can, so the Circle of Love expands in our world.

It's about accepting and being with what is, and somehow see it as "perfect." Using those glasses to look within, one can also find the flawless, innocent, perfect self, in all its magnificence. I have been able to see it and then hold myself with love and compassion. That's the only way I can turn around and give the same to a world that is also hurting and that doesn't seem to understand. Making peace with myself and life, shifting from helplessness to persistence, from confusion to knowing, from judgment to self-compassion, from despair to celebration.

It's also about using those glasses to find the little pieces of light which, at times, are imperceptible. In those dark hours, once I have found them, many times I have tried very hard to hold on to those little pieces, just to see them slip through my fingers. So were they not real? Then, in the midst of my frustration, I pause and remember to take deep breaths, feel whatever I am feeling, and allow Grace to step in through the cracks of my broken heart. The true gift of those little pieces of light has been to shine, allowing me to see where I am and where I need to go and let go, as I feel the calling to flow with life.

As life flows, we learn that nothing is forever, that the only thing that remains constant is change. And yes, I, like many others, have been living a very intense experience of this. Lately, I have felt that my life is falling apart. The goodbyes have not stopped; in fact, I've had to issue one after another to many of those with whom I have been closest—who have loved me most and whom I have most loved. Friends are going away. Doors are closing. Cycles are ending. But beginnings creep in.

As I write this, my little dog Perrito is lying by my side, with seemingly little life left. I know that I will be interrupted countless times while I try to sense if there is anything he needs as he's getting ready to finally lift himself up, shake his ears out, and dutifully cross the Rainbow Bridge to a world that I sense is as beautiful, colorful, and peaceful as his lifelong contribution to me and my family. Needless to say, I am hurting inside even as I honor the gifts he has given us. People around me are wondering if it's a good idea to let things run their course. And the answer is yes, it is. Not because I don't want to let him go, but because I want to honor his desire to live. His determination to hang onto life with whatever strength he has left has been for me both a gift and a huge lesson.

It has been interesting to notice the parallels between the experiences with my husband and my little dog—the common denominator being unconditional love. I am caretaking again, I am appreciating again, I am witnessing an ironclad will to live, combined with a sweet surrender, the same kind of surrender I gracefully undergo as I feel the tides of life shift my soul yet again.

Grace has also been allowing me to see, witness, and sincerely submit myself to the cycle of death and rebirth. I live in Houston, Texas, a large city growing larger by the day. In the past couple of years, I have watched homes and buildings being razed—just like parts of my life—turning into vacant spaces pregnant with possibilities—just like parts of my life—and have watched beautiful, majestic structures slowly take their place—as will hopefully happen within my own life. Right now, it's all about going on and rebuilding. I trust that this period will soon be over. That I will don those grace-full rose-colored glasses and author the next chapter of my life, with a compass of joy guiding me to the resources I need. Grace will give me the inspiration and motivation to embrace my fears and boldly take the next steps as I follow my heart.

And for all this, I am deeply grateful.

May you see through your own rose-colored glasses, finding yourself living "the gift."

ABOUT THE AUTHOR: Originally from Mexico City, where she obtained her CPA degree, Beatriz moved to Houston to advance her professional career with a major international accounting firm. Personal health challenges led her to develop an interest in the body-mind-emotions-spirit connection. Since becoming Nationally Certified in Therapeutic Massage and Bodywork, she has received many certifications in the health, wellness, and personal development fields. Her passion is to share the resources she has found to be helpful in her own journey with others—including the Spanish-speaking population—to help them heal and be empowered to lead joyful, meaningful lives.

Beatriz Schriber
beatrizschriber.com
beschriber@gmail.com
713-417-2332

The Baker's Dozen
Sue Urda

Summer of 1974, I officially joined the workforce at Pizza-n-Subs in the Valley View Center mall in Dallas, Texas. I was more than excited to finally be able to earn some money doing something other than babysitting. Although I had been watching kids for a few years, since I was twelve years old, it wasn't something I really enjoyed. Sure, there were good points—it was easy work, and some of the kids were pretty darn cute and fun to play with, and they seemed to like me well enough. And I really loved to be handed cash at the end of the night.

But the best thing, hands down, was that there was no adult supervision; I got to make my own decisions, like to watch whatever I wanted on TV after the kids went to bed. I remember many times being "scared to death" watching Twilight Zone or Alfred Hitchcock movies and sitting with my back glued to the couch, even afraid to get up and pee, and then jumping up when the couple came home. So, maybe the scary shows weren't such a great decision on my part, but it was *my decision* to make.

Firsts

I also had a couple of "firsts" while babysitting, like flipping through "The Joy of Sex" book and looking through a Playboy magazine. My mom would have flipped if she knew I had access to these, but being raised in a Catholic household, if I hadn't seen it then I don't know when I would have. So I guess I'm grateful for the insights.

One time I got to handle a small emergency when one of the kids fell and cut his head open above his eye. I learned that I was quick to act, methodically did all the things I was "trained" to do, kept the kid calm, and didn't break down until it was under control and he was in his parents' arms. If I remember right, they gave me an extra ten bucks too. Yep, to this day, I am good in a crisis.

My favorite babysitting first was that I got to try new snacks; you know, the things my mother wouldn't buy or I didn't get to eat because one of my four siblings ate them first. There were all different kinds of cookies, chips, and ice cream, and as a hormonal young teen and a food lover this was great stuff!

Pizza - n - Subs

Back to the pizza place... I was a sophomore in high school and begged my parents to get a job. At the time I was only fourteen and the state required us to be fifteen to have a job. I don't remember exactly how I did it—if I lied on my application, if the restaurant manager looked the other way, or what—all I know is that I had a job and I was thrilled!

Not only did I have a job, but for me, it was the best job in the world. It was in the mall and I could shop on my breaks. It was at a pizza place and pizza was then, and still remains, one of my favorite foods. To top it off my best friend got a job there too. In my eyes, this was awesome!

It was here at the pizza place that I had another "first"—one of my co-workers tried to force himself on me. I remember the night clearly. He and I were the only ones there closing up shop and the front gate was pulled down and locked. He opened a small bottle of whiskey, mixed it with Coke, and we drank as we were cleaning up. He was cute and we had kissed a few times in the past; in fact, he taught me how to "suck like a vacuum" when French-kissing for a more intimate experience. And so I didn't think much of it when he reached his arms around me from behind and started to kiss my neck while I had my hands in the soapy water with the greasy pizza pans.

His kisses were tickling me and I knew my dad was coming to pick me up so I resisted his advances and told him to get back to mopping the floor so we could finish up—but he wouldn't stop. He pressed his pelvis into me, grabbed me by the shoulders and turned me around. What had seemed kind of fun and innocent enough a moment ago now felt scary as he pressed his pelvis insistently into mine. I resisted and pulled away, only to see that he had unbuckled his belt, unzipped his pants, and his penis was in full view. I looked into his eyes and asked *What are you doing?* The look on his face said it all. The next thing I knew I had kneed him in the groin hard enough that he screeched and dropped to the greasy floor writhing in pain. I grabbed my coat and purse, and ran down the back hallway, through the mall, and out to the parking lot.

I never mentioned this "first" to anyone because I was too embarrassed and in some way felt responsible. I knew I didn't intend for any of it; in my mind we were just "kissin' friends." I had many conversations with myself about this over the coming few months and decided I had done nothing wrong and was in the clear. I felt grateful for the valuable lesson I learned (and hopefully taught him) and I vowed that I'd never let that happen to me again—and it never did.

Forty-One and a Half Years

So, this was the beginning of forty-one and a half years of trading my time and services for money. When I think about the many hours I have devoted to this common part of everyday life I wonder if it's been worth it.

We can never get back all those hours. We can't go back and undo our choices, we can only take our experience, what we've learned and our relationships, and move forward.

Before becoming an entrepreneur in 1989 when I joined my father in his newly started business, I had jobs at ten other companies. All of them graced me with a distinct knowing about what I wanted to do with my life and career—either by showing me aspects I loved about them or, more often than not, showing me what I definitely did *not* want as I moved forward.

In college I had jobs as an Orientation Counselor and worked in the cafeteria. My favorite job though was as a Resident Assistant in my dorm. I felt good about helping to pay my room and board in this way, as well as giving me some beer, gas, and pizza money. Besides I got my own room and a phone that was paid for—no more sitting on the floor in the hallway chatting on the pay phone for me. It also afforded me privacy, which is scarce in a college dorm.

Summer jobs between semesters were my favorite because I worked as a waitress. It was here that I learned the difference between working for hourly pay and working for tips. I learned that my tips grew in direct proportion to the service I provided. When I was friendly and attentive, thought ahead of the customers' needs, and went the extra mile, I was rewarded—with cash! What a concept. No taxes taken out, no questions asked, I left every day with a wad of cash!

Fall 1981, I spent a semester at university in Wroxton, England. Because it was part of education, my folks said they would pay for it as long as I earned my own spending money. I was on it! The summer before I left I cashed in the many savings bonds I had accumulated over the years and worked three jobs.

One of the three jobs was with UPS where I loaded the trucks on the night shift for the next day's delivery. The packages would come barreling down the conveyor belt landing at my feet and bumping into my legs. After the first week I counted fifty-two bruises on my legs and so I gave that one up after only two weeks. To date, that was one of the highest paying jobs per hour I had and I was grateful for the extra money.

My time in England ended up being an "emotional growth spurt" for me, because my best friend at the time ended up backing out and I felt pretty lonely there at first. It was also a physical growth spurt and not in a good way. I gained thirty pounds in three months eating and drinking my way through pubs and castles. I traded clothes with one of the other girls there because apparently she'd lost the thirty pounds I gained! I even got a "punk" haircut. When I arrived home and walked in the door, my mom came to hug and kiss me, followed by my grandma. Grandma laughed and said, "Don't worry, your hair will grow and you'll lose weight." My mom promptly smacked her in the arm and hugged me again. We made plans to go clothes shopping so I had something to wear for Christmas.

I wouldn't trade that experience for anything. The time away from my "regular college life" opened my eyes to what it would be like after college, to make new friends, and be open to all kinds of people.

The Real World

My four jobs after college before becoming an entrepreneur each graced me with some valuable lessons. My first "real job" out of college was as an Assistant Manager with Macy's (which was then Bamberger's). Here I learned to depend on and take advice from seasoned professionals whose position it was to work for me. At twenty-two years old with a staff averaging forty I learned this one pretty fast; and thank goodness, because in my next few management positions my staff had many more years of industry experience than me. I earned their respect by respecting them and being open to their wisdom.

My waitressing experience came in handy when I went to work as a Placement Specialist—or as many people called my position, a Head Hunter. This job was commission only and my income was totally dependent on my commitment, service, and work ethic, so I went right to work.

Sometimes not knowing enough and being naive helps you open doors you never even would have knocked on, and so I would cold call almost anyone. I signed on two pretty sizeable accounts, one of them because I didn't know enough to be afraid to cold call the V.P. of Finance and Accounting at Exxon. His secretary put me through to him with my first call and I got an immediate appointment. Since I was new to my position, I was accompanied to the meeting by Betsy, my close friend and the Assistant Manager. We were ecstatic when they signed a contract with us. We even got to take the two Exxon V.P.s out to a $200 lunch. Mind you, this was 1985, so this was a lot of money (and a lot of alcohol), all covered by our company. It was great fun and so very satisfying to have my work, enthusiasm, confidence, and a lot of luck translate into a nice paycheck. My first year there I nearly doubled my annual income compared to my previous job, and I felt rich and on track!

The Baker's Dozen

It ends up that being an entrepreneur is actually my thirteenth and final "job." Yep, this is the final one for me. The past twenty-seven years of being my own boss have afforded me many pleasures as well as sleepless nights. I have met amazing people and created beautiful relationships—each of them helping me to grow, oftentimes in ways I didn't even know I needed to.

Unbeknownst to me, the headhunting job as well as the whole dozen of the ones I had prior to becoming an entrepreneur prepared me in ways I could never have planned, and it was my many firsts along the way that molded me to the woman I am today.

It is grace that taught me to have faith in the unknown, to trust and have confidence in what I know is right for me.

Too, grace taught me to be caring, attentive, and open to peoples' needs—and more than that, to intuit them.

Grace keeps me on fire, even through the tough times, even when I feel uncertain, and even when I feel stuck in the muck.

And it is grace that keeps me grateful and happy as I navigate this ever-evolving journey of entrepreneurship and, even more important, the journey of my life.

ABOUT THE AUTHOR: Sue Urda is your Feel Good Guidess. She is an Award-Winning and #1 Bestselling Author, Speaker, Inspirer, and Co-Founder of Powerful You! Women's Network & Powerful You! Publishing. Sue is a two-time honoree in The Inc. 500 America's Fastest-Growing Private Companies. Having started three companies since 1989, Sue knows the challenges and joys businesses face, and she is committed to helping entrepreneurs and all women thrive, get connected, share their stories, and feel good. Sue loves assisting individuals in their own pursuit of success, purposeful-living, and freedom, and her mission is to connect women to each other, their visions, and themselves.

Sue Urda
Feel Good Guidess
Co-Founder of Powerful You! Inc.
powerfulyou.com
powerfulyoupublishing.com

Stranded in a Foreign Country
C. Diane Rivers

Saturday, June 8, 1996—the day I married my soul mate Michael—was one of the most joyful of my life! After a wonderful honeymoon in Naples, Florida, we returned home to New Jersey to start our new life. Just two weeks later, I received an incredible call from my employer. Was I interested in working in the Bahamas for a year? A company had heard about my ability to teach doctors, physician's assistants, nurses, and coders to run their practices profitably and they wanted me there to train medical professionals on Abaco Isle and other islands. She had barely asked the question when I was mentally packing my bags. Of course, Michael and I discussed this, had our attorney look over the contract, met the owners, and saw slides of the beautiful island. As we drank wine and laughed about how great this new endeavor was going to be a win-win for everyone, I kept thinking, *"What a Blessing."* That was July and we were due to depart on September 5.

At our final meeting in August, the company gave more details about my monthly payments, which would be wired into an account. We were also given a two-bedroom house, a car, a small canoe, and a bike to ride around the island. Cool! My husband had to sign papers stating he would not work; the arrangement was for my services only and he would risk deportation for both of us if he took a job. No worries there, we said, since the salary—thirty-five dollars per hour—was in the mid-nineties considered pretty good. A week before our departure date, we packed our wedding gifts and must haves; we left our homes and cars to others and with our round trip tickets supplied by the company we began our adventure.

Once we landed a very uncomfortable feeling came over me, but I tried to fight it and didn't say anything to Michael. We were met at the airport by a woman who introduced herself as the owner of the company's sister. She was friendly and I told myself the feeling was wrong, but I could no longer deny it when we got to our destination. The house we were promised was actually a dilapidated shack! The sister got out, went inside and literally dragged her ninety-year-old mother and mentally challenged fifty-year-old sister out of the house we were supposed to live in. Michael and I watched, horrified. There are no words to describe this dramatic scene with the mother and daughter, who cursed us for putting them out of their home. We told the sister to please put us in a hotel until we could figure this out. Nope, she stated, this was the agreement; besides, no hotels on the island had vacancies. That was the beginning of our living nightmare. We walked into the house to find it infested with mosquitoes, flying palmetto bugs, and sugar ants. Still Michael and I tried to make the best of it. We can manage, we said, it's only one year. But it only got worse; no hot water, no cable, no electricity after 11pm. There was no car; the bike had only one wheel, and the canoe was rusted through. It was beyond believing.

Perhaps even worse was the way the island people treated us—with complete disdain. From day one they were very rude to us, even when we attempted to buy food, services or goods. The first week there we thought we would treat ourselves to dinner at one of their fancy restaurants. Although the place was empty, we stood waiting to be seated for at least for fifteen minutes. No one appeared. Then a white couple came up behind us waiting to be seated as well. Immediately, and as if out of thin air, a waiter appeared and asked them where they wanted to sit?

When the couple pointed out that we were there first, the waiter looked as us and said, "What do you want?"

"Nothing apparently," we said and walked out, as did the white couple, much to the waiter's protest.

Contrary to what we had been told, EVERYONE on the island had cars but us! No one rode a bike. By the way, the bike had one tire and was so rusty from the weather it wouldn't move. The canoe was rotten with a big hole. And despite our efforts the house remained crawling with bugs. We had to sleep in shifts—literally. They had no hospitals, no movies, no mall, and no downtown. There was no animal control either, and wild dogs, goats and boars roamed freely through the streets. The worst thing for me, though, was that there was no beach. That's right—an island with no beach! The trees went right down into the ocean except where they had boats docked. The two hotels had beaches, but they were for guests only.

Then there was the job itself. I worked every day except Sunday, and when it was time to get my first monthly paycheck, guess what? It was not in the account! No big deal, I thought, my next month check will be double. Trust and Faith is a part of my makeup. After training started; the company realized the whole island needed help. So I taught evenings and weekends to anyone who had the time or desire to learn Windows. It wasn't like I didn't need the money. The "pretty good" salary wasn't so good compared with the cost of living on the island. One roll of toilet paper cost five dollars.

In the coming months we kept reminding ourselves to stay positive and that this wasn't forever. In October we were hit by our first hurricane. Very, very, scary, a lot of flooding, loss of power, and lot of prayers.

In November, there was still no money, just a lot of excuses. Calling the U.S. was an ordeal, wired communication wasn't any better, and complaining to my attorney was fruitless. We just had to trust that everything would work out. In the meantime, we had to live off our credit cards for the entire month of November. One night, after a stressful fight with Michael about our finances, I decided to take a walk and was chased by a huge wild goat. I thank God/Grace that Michael had unknowingly followed me.

Add to this, that we almost got deported after Michael accepted a job at a hotel. Immigration found out and sent authorities to Abaco to arrest us! We were so grateful for the friendship of one of the doctors, who allowed us to hide in her home a few days until they left. We discovered then that the company never advertised the job to Bahamians. The islanders felt that an American had taken it away from one of their own. Finally, we knew why they hated us!

By the end of November, we had no more money on our credit cards, no more savings, and no income! It was definitely time to go. We packed what we had, six giant bags of clothing and wedding gifts, then stopped at a local store and picked up the Miami Herald.

When the storekeeper asked if we were going home, we both looked at each other and started to cry! We had nowhere to go—people were already living in our homes back in New Jersey. Stunned at our reaction, he wrote down the name of a friend in North Palm Beach. We thanked him, not having a clue what he was talking about or where in the heck North Palm Beach was.

Again, Grace was our guide and Faith our path. After a harrowing return flight to the States, we literally kissed the ground. The Customs Agents were friendly and smiling, in fact, everyone we saw was friendly and smiling throughout the airport; it warmed our hearts. After months of outright rudeness, we were so glad to be back in America! No matter that we only had eighty dollars borrowed from friends—we were home. We found happiness in a cheap hotel, hot water, and a hot meal. We woke up to catch the connecting flight and Michael said, "*I am not getting on another plane.*"

What? Excuse me! We have tickets that are already paid for to get us back to New Jersey. Nope, his fear of crashing was so great there was no debate or persuasion. We missed the flight. We had no idea where the Gifts of Grace and Gratitude would take us. We were homeless. We were fragile, scared, broke… and yet we were trusting. Trusting that Grace would carry us through if we just stayed open to Faith.

I cannot even begin to share the multitude of miracles that took place in our life from that point on. The first was being able to pay just five dollars for Greyhound bus tickets to take us anywhere in Florida. Talk of living with my youngest sister, Tawanna in Dallas or my sister Dolores in North Carolina went out the window. Michael said NO! All of a sudden that piece of paper that was scribbled on from the Bahamian storekeeper came out of nowhere. SEE JOEY IN NORTH PALM BEACH AT ECONOLODGE. No phone number, but okay, North Palm Beach here we come. As we soon found out though, Greyhound didn't go to North Palm Beach, only West Palm Beach, about fifteen miles away. We got off the bus and looked at each other. We didn't even have enough money for a cab ride! Now, it's dark and cool out; we're in a strange deserted place by the intercostal, and all I could think as I looked at the full moon on the water, was how beautiful this town was. How safe I felt. Grace is everywhere, and we had Gratitude for that! An hour later, a cab pulled up and asked us where we were headed, EconoLodge, North Palm Beach, we told him, but we had no money. He said hop in. Thank you God! Once there we asked for Joey, wondering if he was even on that night. The desk clerk told us to have a seat in the lobby, which we did for over an hour. Finally the clerk said "You know what? Joey should be here soon but just in case, why not wait for him in one of the rooms and just relax?" He gave us a key and we took our bags into a nice little room with a king-sized bed and waited. Suddenly, there was a banging on the door that jolted us out of our skin.

"Who is it"? Michael called out.

"Joey."

At that point we looked at each other, wondering, did we really want to see Joey? Michael opened the door to this huge intimidating man! Oh no, not again. More anger and hatred! He stood there and wanted to know why we asked for him. He listened as we explained our dilemma, then he left, slamming the door behind him. Now we're thinking, how do we get out of here? Fearful in this strange town with strange people, we began to pray for protection, comfort and guidance. Suddenly, this indescribable feeling of peace settled over us.

Joey came back, but what a different man he seemed; instead of that towering figure of six feet six-inches, we saw a humble apologetic soul in front of us. Joey was from the Bahamas! Abaco was his home and he had been the Deputy of Chiefs there for years. He called the island and found out what we said to be true; he also apologized for how his people treated us. He explained as owner of the EconoLodge he had come across a lot of con artists and thought we were the same. Now, he offered us unlimited stayed at this beautiful resort motel in North Palm Beach—even took us out to dinner that night. He helped us learn the bus system, put us in touch with a branch of Avis rental owned by a friend of his who only charged us five dollars a week for a brand new Toyota Corolla. We also reached out to my brother Mikal's mother-in-law, who happened to live just one mile south of us. She was a huge help, with showing us how to get jobs—in fact our very first holiday in Florida was Thanksgiving at her house. We felt Blessed! Our plan was to work and save money to return home in June because we really missed our grandkids. We have the deepest Gratitude that those plans never materialized. Twenty years later, we still live here in Florida—now with several of the kids, grandkids, and great grandkids!

The company never paid us, and when we attempted to sue we learned they had declared bankruptcy. Years ago it seemed like suffering, but we didn't know the whole adventure was a way to keep us happily married and more compassionate toward others. We have the returned flight tickets framed by our wedding picture—a reminder to always be grateful for life's grace-full detours!

ABOUT THE AUTHOR: Diane is an author, Healing Touch and Beyond Surgery practitioner, and Holistic Counselor specializing in stress and grief care. She holds bachelor's degrees in Psychology and Education. For the past sixteen years she has facilitated healing through her program, *Shift It Thru Energy Medicine.* Diane also offers monthly *Ignite Your Life* sessions that share various healing energy modalities to reduce stress and pain and gain clarity, focus, and energy. Diane is also the author of *Theodore Turns 5*, a children's storybook and coloring book about friendship. Diane has been happily married for twenty years and is the proud mother of seven children, four grandchildren, and four great-grandchildren.

C. Diane Rivers
Shift It thru Energy Medicine
tothegoldwithin.com
cdivadi@yahoo.com
561-351-2100

Grace Will Lead Me Home
Marilen Crump

"GOD, I am mad at you!"

I was lost and feeling deeply depressed. I couldn't understand my life anymore. Nothing made sense. I was alone and seeking ways to make a final cry that would end all the sorrow and heartbreak. I made a defiant trip to a nearby store. *My last act will be full of symbolism*, I morbidly chuckled inside my head. My hand grabbed a wine bottle with the name GHOST PINES as I proceeded to another aisle to find sleep medication. I anticipated maybe a little suspicion from the checkout girl but there was no reaction to my toxic purchase. *How can people not feel my aching pain or not notice the dried tears on my face?* I wondered.

The drive to my secret place of solitude was beautiful and serene. My mind was anything but. I was spinning in extreme turmoil. I pulled my wits together enough to write a short note to my children: *I love you both so much with all my heart and soul. I am very sorry for any pain I've caused you.* It felt wrong and I knew it. Anger can be a good way to squelch the guilt and I resolved to continue my warped mission. The river would be my way out—no more pain, no more debt, no more disappointments… NO MORE ME.

I cycled through many emotions of hurt, anger, and sadness, but when hope would try to bubble up—I would quickly start to sob again to draw my sadness back to the surface. I recollected the first big pain I had in life, which centered around my first serious relationship in high school. I convinced myself that I can blame him too for my broken spirit—along with my college boyfriend and soon-to-be ex-husband, and everyone else who had taken me for granted. I pulled together a mix of rage and pain and dialed the first boyfriend's number. When he answered I did not hesitate to express aloud my disappointments and my pain. I shared with him that the inevitable was coming and I would be saying my final goodbyes. I wanted him to suffer, but not stop me. If he tried to find or stop me, I warned, or call anyone else, I would DEFINITELY do it and it would really be his fault.

He was much calmer than I expected. My tears were dripping steadily onto the ground. He spoke of how sorry he was for the past and for how I felt now. He said that I was too special, a mother, and that I should not give up, if only for the sake of the kids. He vowed he would not stop me but would keep hoping and praying that I find a way to feel better. It was then that a shadow started to darken my blurred vision. I picked my head up to observe a large cloud hovering over me. I cried harder after seeing that the cloud was in the shape of a large heart. This sign would be one of the many gifts of GRACE that GOD would send that day and the days to follow.

GRACE would send a loving friend who reached out and hunted me down to rescue me from my isolated location. I slowly let my heart fill with hope because a strong feeling of guidance started pulling on me. I sought out a way to connect with GOD and felt compelled to attend a nearby church. I tentatively entered the doors and immediately a chatty teenager named Jeremy approached me. He wrapped his arm around my shoulder as if he knew me, then escorted me to a seat. After the service he repeatedly asked me if I was going to come back. I don't remember anything the pastor spoke of that day, nor do I remember any other part of the experience other than the young man who made me feel guilty if I did not return. I did go back again, and the music seeped into my soul. I just wanted to thank the choir after the service but the director actually asked me to join them. *She hasn't even heard me sing*, I thought to myself, yet I felt welcomed and nurtured by such a warm invitation. The GRACE of this choir and church community would become a source of new joy and community for me.

Grace & Discovery

I credit the mystery of unexpected GRACE for turning me into a seeker. I started observing people around me and the relationships they had. I asked tons of questions. I knew that there was an answer waiting for me out there. I began to think of future possibilities and started to ask myself honest questions... *What did I really want? What can I offer a new partner? What do I need to change about myself?* I grabbed a small journal and charted out a new husband. I knew that my heart really wanted it, but I realized that I never asked the Lord for someone that would be my perfect fit. I ordered up a very specific person down to the point of what he liked to eat and even that he would love my cats!

I used that chart to help me navigate life when meeting a potential date. He would have to be everything on the list. I didn't care if it was a tall and impossible order. I would rather be alone than to fall back into the old traps of my life again.

I began to cheer myself up by doing things I loved. Going to karaoke would be one of those things. I had to try to put myself out there, but on my terms. One fateful evening a handsome stranger approached me and simply complimented my singing. We exchanged some information and yet it was another month before our paths crossed again and we made plans to see each other.

This man spoke differently to me than the typical person. He said words like Meditation, Frequency, and Gratitude. He told me that we had the responsibility to stay positive and *monitor our thoughts,* and how we had more control over our world than we allow ourselves to have. It was eye-opening and I wanted to absorb every bit of it!

He lived what he spoke and I admired him for it. I had a lot of negative thoughts to correct and at times it would be frustrating. He was very patient. After six months of dating, I happened upon my chart, which I had completely forgotten about and was hesitant to look at it—in case he did not meet all my specifications.

Miracles & Gratitude

It was a definite relief that Kenny matched my chart one hundred percent. My heart felt lighter and my soul more connected to my hopes and my dreams. I was thankful! My tears were no longer flowing, but my sense of wonder of just how grand things can become was what pulled me through each day. I smiled more and gratitude became a powerful tool to ward off the distressed emotions. Gratitude became a new habit for me, just like breathing, and I wanted to inspire others with this amazing process.

I had a business named ARTINSPIRED that I originally named as a catchy term to describe the theme of my photography work, but I began to envision it as a new resource for others. I began to create a space for inspiration, and a center to engage others in positive thinking, gratitude and goal-setting. ARTINSPIRED is a place where they can safely overcome adversities and discover empowerment and fun.

When I look back at that spirit-breaking experience, I am thankful for every part of it. My transformation had to begin at the bottom where my pride had to be stripped from me.

I now recognize that GRACE is such an amazing part of life and it blesses those who may not even be seeking it or deserving of it. It generates GRATITUDE in me as if the frequency of my thankfulness is a way for me to communicate with the spirit of grace and give it a hug. And finally to GOD, the creator of GRACE, I just want to say, "THANK YOU GOD for everything you have done to bring me to such peace and abundance. I love you and I am happy to be your servant of goodwill!"

ABOUT THE AUTHOR: Marilen Crump is a graduate of Sweet Briar College in Virginia and is the owner of ArtInspired (est. 2000) which provides self-development in areas of Art, Movement, Wellness and Inspiration. ArtInspired has partnered with Todd Health & Wellness and Harvest of Health to create the PERSONAL EVOLUTION GUILD ™, *A New Way to Engage, Innovate and Strategize Improvements in Your Life.* Marilen is a polymath in the areas of ballroom dancing, photography, public speaking, vocalist, poetry and other artistic pursuits. She finds great satisfaction in collaboration, coaching and spending quality time with her husband Ken and their five children.

Marilen Crump
ArtInspired, LLC
ARTINSPIRED.com
artinspiredme@gmail.com
757-768-9033

Love Versus Fear
Alexa Person

Standing in line at the grocery, lunch in hand, my cell phone began "glitching" and within a few minutes it was completely inoperable. Inundated with business and clients, it wasn't a convenient time to be wrangling with failing tech, but I shook my head and chuckled. I wasn't about to let this affect me.

Rifling through my desk, I found an old cell phone and powered it up. Although it was much smaller and slower than what I was used to, it did the job and I was grateful, but it would soon deliver a surprise.

As I attempted to send a text, a new one popped up. It was from my ex-husband, who was hundreds of miles away: "If you're home, please pay the gardener." Stunned, I sat in my car starring at it. What the hell was he talking about? Where was I? What was going on? For a fleeting moment, I was married and back in our house. Seeing his old text literally compressed time.

Quickly scanning the rest of my phone, I was involuntarily led down memory lane. Photos, emails, and notes, all filled with my life from that era, were brutally intact. Even my "favorites" call list was waiting for me, my ex-husband being first, of course. Realizing it was the workings of an old SIM card rather than a moment from the *Twilight Zone,* I shook it off, sent my text, and got on the road.

I was en route to my cousin, Dr. Ralph Person's Celebration of Life Memorial at The University of Texas Alumni Center. Ralph was President of the U.T. Student Body, a track star, and a head of the Theology Dept. He later received a PhD and became a Presbyterian Minister. He was a learned, enlightened, and loving soul.

His family had planned an incredible event in his honor. And it didn't hurt that my cousin's husband, Gary Powell, was in charge of the music. As the head of the U.T. Music Dept. and an Emmy-nominated composer whose work has sold millions of albums worldwide, his program was amazing. Equally moving were the tributes. And as a clairvoyant, I was honored to experience many beautiful moments beyond the veil, which I later shared privately.

After the memorial, we poured out into the foyer where we visited, noshed and paid tribute to Ralph. It truly was a celebration of life and no one wanted to leave! The staff literally broke down the event around us as we chatted and dug for apps off the covered trays. But immediately after I left things got bumpy, again.

Moments after the event, I found myself sitting in the lobby of the very same hotel where I was married years ago. It was the last time my family and I had gathered together in Austin, and Ralph officiated. As my physical body feigned a smile and engaged in polite conversation, my mind experienced the wedding all over again and I felt the heartache of my divorce plunge into my heart, but why?

Our dinner reservation quickly approached, so I went to my room and dropped off my bag. As I put my luggage down, I noticed a small stuffed bunny sitting awkwardly in the middle of the bed. It seemed out of place. I didn't have time to give it much thought. Instead, I turned to freshen up, where I was again met with more surprises.

On the counter, neatly fanned-out, were a number of baby products, bath toys and a bib. My heart fell when I realized why a curious stuffed animal sat on my bed. The hotel was not aware of my divorce and hadn't changed my profile. When I made my reservation they assumed I would be arriving with my husband and his toddler. Waves of sadness rose within me, but I stuffed them down. Late, I dashed out the door and pulled myself together.

The streets of Austin were a welcome relief. The Gay Pride Parade was in full swing! Our restaurant was on a second floor and we had a perfect rooftop view. Grateful for the distraction, I took full advantage of our vista to beam Love into thousands of strangers. But the thing about distractions is they're always short-lived. Sooner or later whatever you're avoiding will come back around with even more force.

Walking back to the hotel, we happened to pass the restaurant where my ex-husband hosted our rehearsal dinner. Looking up, I noticed the signage had changed. For more than a decade it has been my favorite restaurant. *And now the owner changed the sign?* It was a small thing, but it weighed heavily upon me. My favorite spot was different now, much like my life and what I expected it to look like.

Feeling raw and vulnerable, I returned to my hotel room and walked past the bed, straight to the windows in order to close the drapes. That's when I saw it. I was in such a rush earlier that I'd completely missed it.

Sitting on the desk was a platter of fresh fruits, cheeses, and a bottle of champagne on ice. I was suddenly starring in a cruel version of *Punk'd*. Gingerly, I reached for the sealed envelope that was perfectly perched atop of two napkins and silverware. The card read: "Mr. and Mrs. Person (at least they used my name) welcome back! We hope you enjoy your stay…" I stopped reading.

My heart doubled over in pain. I couldn't speak. Tears flowed as I felt the loss of my marriage all over again. But why was I in so much pain? I couldn't understand it. I'd already been through all this! I'd spent almost a year in agony to prove it!

As I tumbled into grief the phone rang. It was my cousin calling to tell me her dear friend suffered a heart attack earlier that afternoon and died. Her need for support released me from my own and I was able to assist her. My service to her became a salve to my freshly reopened wounds. It was early morning before my head hit the pillow.

Mid-morning, I gazed at my disheveled reflection in the mirror and wondered how I would garner the energy to get through my day. I was a guest speaker at Pat Imholte's Sacred Heart Workshop later that afternoon. It was my first official talk, but my eyes were swollen and I radiated exhaustion. Centering myself, I asked my Family of Light to fill me with the Love and Light I required to work through my resurrected sadness and be of service to everyone attending the workshop.

A few hours later, I was dressed, enjoyed a lovely brunch and was en route to my talk. I was tired, but given the circumstances, I wasn't nearly as tired as I could have been. My Guides had filled me with the Light I needed to ease my fatigue, for which I was incredibly grateful.

Arriving on time for my appearance, I was received with the

Love that had escaped me hours before. With renewed spirit, I gave an overview for my new book and workshops and then Pat conducted her own workshop.

While Pat spoke, the energy I normally work with filled my body and poured out into the room and toward Pat. Pat suddenly stopped speaking and said: "He wants to speak." She then went on to channel Jesus and give us each an individualized message.

Yeshua's message to me wasn't a surprise: "balance" and "be happy." I wondered how I would make that happen. My new book, workshops, and all they entailed had consumed the last ten months of my life. As far as "balance" went, I didn't have any. And the "be happy" part was a challenge. I just said goodbye to my cousin who happened to have married me, yet the marriage was gone and I experienced one of the most emotional nights of my life.

Pat finished delivering Jesus's message and returned to her seat. What happened next was a surprise to all of us. As she sat solemnly with her palms facing upward, Jesus asked for someone to accept His energy and act as a channel for Pat. He wanted to give *her* a message.

I remained in my seat, waiting to see if someone else would be called, but no one answered. After a few moments, a participant near me whispered: "Alexa, please go." I knew I was to do it, but I was apprehensive. Just as Jesus was about to leave I came out of my interdimensional haze and jumped out of my seat.

Placing my hands on her head, I closed my eyes and waited. Nothing happened immediately, but suddenly I felt my body taking deep, deliberate breaths. The sound surprised me and I realized my body was inhaling as much oxygen as possible in order to maintain consciousness. I soon felt the dizzying waves of an intense, high frequency, golden-white energy enter my body. It spun through me, consuming me as I stood before her. Through blinding Light, I felt my consciousness become a part of a massive energy wave. Through Love, faith and surrender I was blended into Yeshua's frequency. His energy was literally blending into my own. In all my years of working directly with Him, I've never Trance-Channeled Him in this way.

Despite the trembling that gripped my body, I delivered Yeshua's message to Pat. As a powerful, yet humble healer dedicated to the service to others, Pat has never been a recipient of her own type of gift. Until that moment, she had never received a message from her Jesus and I was incredibly honored and grateful to act as a conduit in her service.

As soon as He finished speaking I felt His energy move out of my body gently, yet quickly. I felt my own consciousness quickly return fully and "snap back." Leaning down, I hugged Pat and tried to return to my seat, but it was too difficult to walk. Rather, I found myself seated on the floor next to her. A kind and loving attendee rushed over to assist in grounding me and I soon stopped shaking enough to walk-crawl back to my seat.

Within moments, I realized His energy was not completely gone and I had somehow been shifted. All the cells in my body were vibrating. The intensity increased and I became very hot, so hot I sweat through my clothes. Fanning myself with the workshop program, I tried not to draw attention to myself as she closed the event.

Looking back, I realize the Universe was asking me to clear the last shard of my unhealed pain. The Cosmos eagerly set in motion specific events (albeit excruciatingly painful ones), which set the stage for me to choose whether or not I would release the last sliver of fear that was locked so deeply within my heart.

The pain I experienced occurred because I was imposing my will on an event, rather than allowing it to unfold. Instead of acting as an observer, being curious, and allowing it to wash over me, I steered it into an outcome where I was met with resistance. Memories on my phone, at the hotel, and the restaurant became increasingly painful due to my own sense of loss and unmet expectations. Every time I wished the events of the past and present were different, rather than allowing them to just "be" and accept the divinity of a larger Universal plan, which I myself set in place, I experienced grief. By attempting to rewrite history, I engaged in a dialogue with my ego and blocked flow from the higher frequencies associated with Unity Consciousness. I couldn't be "One" with the Universe when I was busy being in a state of separation, which is fear.

On the contrary, I experienced resistance-free moments while I was acting in service to my cousin and others in the workshop. When I was in flow, allowing the Universe to co-create with my consciousness, outside of ego, there was no resistance. Thus, I was in flow when I was in service to others.

The world you occupy and everything within it is a projection of your own consciousness. You created this stage for your education and for the sake of expanding your soul into Love. The frequency you align with is entirely up to you. Fear is the lowest frequency and Love is the highest octave. Choose Love.

Lean into your fear fully and shake hands with your pain because true growth takes place when you work through all the gifts of your challenges. And even when you think you've dealt with it all, it's quite possible a fissure lingers deep within you.

The only way to grow and assimilate the new conscious-accelerating energy is to heal the obstacles impeding its path. And if you allow it, your shadow self can assist in illuminating the Light within you.

Walk in Love and Faith and Surrender into your Light by facing your fears, healing your pain, serving others, and being grateful for it all.

ABOUT THE AUTHOR: Alexa Person was born "awake" and gifted with the full spectrum of clairvoyant gifts. As an Alchemist of Light, she is committed to shifting individuals into a higher alignment of their own Divine Male-Female frequency. Alexa holds a B.A. in Art History from SMU in Dallas and has produced award-winning films with her partners at Aristar Entertainment and Packin' Heat Pictures. Alexa's regular public speaking engagements include her work as a Medium and a Certified Akashic Records Consultant. A committed philanthropist, Alexa has served on Boards of Directors and Special Committees in Texas for over fifteen years.

Alexa Person
Alchemist of Light
alexaperson.com

A Charmed Life

Filomena Concia

Two weeks ago, I called my best friend Pamela to tell her that the tumor on my lung had been reduced to a scar.

After some heartfelt love and congratulations, she said, "You live a charmed life, my friend."

A charmed life? Really? It felt as though I'd been struggling through this life for as long as, well, as long as I've been living it. Sure, there had been many joyful moments and things that had gone my way, but *charmed*? Her words gave me pause, so I decided to take another look from a different perspective. Hmm...there had been a lot of "coincidences" and miraculous saves all along the way. Suddenly I remembered a "Healing the Inner Child" exercise I did with a dear friend twelve years earlier. Through hypnosis I was able to "visit" myself as a very young child. I told her, "Everything is going to be okay; I'm here to help you now." She looked at me, smiled, and said "I know who you are; you're my angel. You're always here." So, was that it? Have I had an angel with me all my life, who helped me survive it all?

It began with my earliest memory: I was about four years old, and my mentally ill alcoholic mother had decided to kill herself, me and my two-year-old sister. She turned on all the gas jets, opened the oven door, and laid down to die. I woke up suddenly, smelled the gas, turned it all off, grabbed my little sister, and went out on the fire escape. When she tried to climb out after us the window slammed shut. We climbed down onto the street, waited until we knew she'd be passed out, and went back inside. What woke me up? Why did the window slam?

About a year later, our neighbor just "happened" to walk in on one of our mother's violent tirades, and called the police. She was sent to the state hospital for four years, and we were adopted by our grandparents.

At the age of 7 I was brutally sodomized by a man I loved and trusted completely, and although I had no recollection of the event, I did develop PTSD. Many years later, under hypnosis, I "saw" the whole thing. At that point I had been spiritually awakened, done all the forgiveness work, and could handle it. And it answered all my questions about certain family relationships and my mysterious allergies and health problems. I know now I was "saved" from going insane, which I surely would have done if I had been conscious of the attack as a kid. Instead, I learned of it at the right time with the right person there to help me. I won't go into all the rest of the child abuse. It's in the past, I've made my peace with it. It didn't start with my abusers; it didn't even start with theirs. What matters is that it ended with me.

That said, I was by no means a perfect mother; in fact, like my mother before me I too became an alcoholic. For twenty-two years I drank myself into oblivion, including the first eight years of my daughter's life, all the while telling myself I was okay because I wasn't "as bad" as the woman who raised me. Still, I was bad enough, doing things that risked my safety – even my life – with no idea that I was being watched over and protected by something much greater than myself.

One night I had an argument in a bar and stormed out. That's the last thing I remember. I woke up the next morning in my car, on the side of a highway; the engine was off, all the doors were locked. I called a friend to find out what happened.

"You stormed out of the bar and went home," he said, "I came by to check on you later, and there was a note on your door saying you were going back to New York."

I checked the mile marker, and drove to the next exit. I had driven 150 miles in a blackout and didn't have a scratch on me.

Rock bottom finally came that New Year's Eve. I was working in a restaurant and had been drinking all night. When the bartender wouldn't sell me my customary six pack to go, I remember being furious—even calling him some choice names—then everything went blank. When I came to work the next day, I learned the rest. I had attacked him, knocked him out with a full bottle of beer, threw a table on top of him, and tried to beat him to death. When others pulled me off him, I proceeded to thoroughly trash the bar, and was then dragged out of there and driven home by a friend. The bartender spent the night in the hospital with a concussion and a lot of bruises. Fortunately, he didn't press charges. At first I didn't believe the story, but when it was confirmed by a close friend, I felt like I'd been kicked in the stomach. I stumbled into the kitchen, held onto the counter for dear life and said out loud, "I can't go on like this. Please, God, help me!" As angry as I was at God at that point in my life (I blamed Him/Her for everything wrong in my life) and as much as I had blasphemed Him/Her, I didn't expect much. But I didn't drink that day, or the next, or—as it turned out—ever again.

I joined a support group of people who were just like me. They helped me stay away from that first drink and look for the underlying causes of my drinking. With their help, I formed a relationship with a Higher Power. It wasn't the same scary, judgmental, punishing God I was brought up with in Catholic school, but a God of my own understanding—kind, loving, and forgiving. And with Him/Her I worked at becoming a person I could love and respect. Over the years, my relationship with my God continued to deepen, and my angels continued to take care of me…even through cancer.

Last winter I caught a very bad cold, with a wracking cough that hurt my ribs and eventually sent me to the ER. They couldn't tell from x-ray whether my ribs were cracked so they gave me something non-narcotic for the pain and sent me home. The next day I got a call from the lab. They had seen a "growth" on my left lung, and wanted me to follow up with a doctor. The next two months brought a series of CAT scans, PET scans, a failed biopsy (they poked a hole in my lung before they got enough material), and visits to a pulmonary doctor and a thoracic surgeon. The final diagnosis: 95% chance it was a cancerous tumor on my lung. The suggested treatment: cut out the tumor, along with a big chunk of my lung. I decided against the surgery, because I needed my lungs to do Transformational Breathwork. My doctors reluctantly said they'd give me six weeks to "do it my way."

I called an old friend who gave me some food grade hydrogen peroxide and super-oxygenated water. Cancer can't live in a super-oxygenated environment. I took the peroxide for a month (the water ran out in a week), but the constant nausea was too much for me, so I stopped. At the same time, another friend showed me where I could get some medical marijuana (I knew they made anti-fungal strains without the THC that gets you high) in capsule form. I took three capsules a day for the next six weeks. The next CAT scan showed a thinning of the tumor. "I don't understand it" said the doctor, "but let's take another one in six weeks." I continued taking the capsules, and six weeks later the tumor was nothing but a scar. Truly confounded, the doctor pointed to the first scan and said, "That's a cancer; that's exactly what cancer looks like." When he got to the second scan, he just shook his head. The third one, he said, "That is a scar, just a scar. I don't like to throw the word miracle around, but this is only the second time in twenty-two years I've ever seen anything like this."

In every aspect of this situation, God, the universe and my angels had conspired to affect a healing. I don't throw the word miracle around either, but to me, this fits the bill.

In my support group we spoke of spiritual awakenings – how they can come in a flash of "knowing" or small "nudges." I have experienced both. Of course there were trials and tribulations along the way; times when my faith waned, and I wandered away from my support group and my daily prayer ritual, only to find myself back in hell. I've heard it said that religion is for people who are afraid to go to hell; spirituality is for people who've already been there. I would add to this, *several times.*

I was ten years sober when my mother died suddenly. Although I had cut her out of my life years earlier, I fell completely apart. There were so many unresolved issues between us; I also felt guilty for leaving my sister alone to deal with her. I maintained my sobriety, but there was no question I still had a lot of work to do.

I had been in and out of shrinks' offices since I was eighteen years old; most of them just patted me on the head, and said, "Oh, you poor thing, no wonder you drink/drank. Here, take these pills." And I went to York Hospital's Cottage, which specializes in substance abuse treatment, and they helped me change my life. My therapist Diane helped me realize that I did love my mother, I was just still afraid of her. Diane also said I had made the right decision by cutting ties, for I'd been taking care of myself and my daughter. Most importantly, she helped me do the forgiveness work I needed so badly to do.

Shortly after my last session I ran into a friend at a dancing boat cruise. I told him how wonderful the group and Diane had been, but that I still felt like "something's stuck inside of me." He handed me a card and said, "This is exactly what you need." It was the phone number for Judith Kravitz at Transformational Breath®. Thus began my fantastic journey with the breathwork.

Words cannot describe how I felt after my first breath session; I can only say that I felt so much lighter and more alive, and like I was in my own body for the first time in my life. After a few more sessions, Judith invited me to take facilitator training as part of a work study program. *Learn to do this for other people? Hell yes!* The training was magical in so many ways, but one thing in particular completely changed my perspective on myself and my life.

It was just before a session and I was telling Liz, one of the trainers, that I wished I could see the "thing" in me that the people who love me see. During the ensuing session, Liz bent down and touched me very lightly. Suddenly I saw this little room that was so beautiful, and colorful, and full of dazzling, bright pulsating light. I shot up and said, "That's what they see!", then burst into tears. After the session, I asked Liz what it was. "It was your soul," she replied, "You were standing at the door to it, but were afraid to open it, so I opened it for you." For a woman who used to think her soul was black and ugly, it was a lot to take in. I spent the rest of that day sobbing tears of gratitude and pure joy.

After the training was over, I started doing breath sessions whenever I could for myself and other people. It is the most gratifying and heartwarming practice I have ever done. Every time I helped another human being to heal, my heart felt lighter, and my soul was brighter. Every single time. I was healing myself right along with them, and I've been grateful for every moment of it.

So, do I live a charmed life? No, Pamela, I live a miraculous life. A life full of love, and God's grace.

There was a nun in my grammar school, whose name, "coincidentally," was Sister Philomena. She had a beautiful, glowing face, and used to give me St. Philomena prayer cards. As she "floated" down the hall, she'd stop, poke my heart gently, and say "God's right there," and "float" off. I'm here to say that she was right. God is in my heart—and in everyone's heart. We just have to look hard enough to find Him/Her, and love enough to keep Him/Her there.

ABOUT THE AUTHOR: Filomena Concia is an author and true Renaissance woman. Born in New York City to an Irish mother and Italian father, she was raised by her maternal grandparents in the Riverdale section of the Bronx. Over the years she has held jobs as a waitress, rural mail carrier, and daycare owner, to name a few. In 1996, she took a course to learn Transformational Breath® and is to this day a practicing Transformational Breath® Facilitator. She has also lived in several states, including New Hampshire, Pennsylvania., Maine, Florida, Arizona, New Jersey, Massachusetts, and Washington. She currently lives in Homer, Alaska.

Filomena Concia
41528 Manson Dr. Apt. B
Homer, AK 99603
907-226-1131

Answering the Call
From Within
dLee

May you have the hindsight to know where you've been, the foresight to know where you are going, and the insight to know when you have gone too far. ~ Irish Blessing

Our lives are like a time track set to railroad ties. If you pay attention, you can feel the motion of it, like a train rocking from side to side as it goes toward its destination. Some of us move at high speed, trying to get "somewhere"; others take a side trip because life has shifted us in a new direction. The interesting thing is that, as each of us moves along this track, our life experiences move along outside us (much like the views through the windows of a train). The question is, are you actively participating in the experience, or are you just watching it all pass by? This alignment (or lack thereof) is important to note because of the profound effect it has on your sense of connectedness with who you are and how you are showing up in your life.

I am a lifelong dreamer, which, as you might imagine, has led to many detours along the way. But whether it's a major leg of my journey or one of my side trips, a great deal of my life has been spent spinning my life experiences into positivity. I learned how to do so at an early age and through consistent exposure from my mother, who spent time each evening reading passages out loud from her favorite book, Norman Vincent Peale's "The Power of Positive Thinking."

As I look back down the track today, I can see that my mother embraced and walked in Grace. I used to think of her as the "ironing board philosopher" (she did a lot of ironing for my family and others). Now I think the repetitive motion it took to convert a wrinkled piece of fabric into a crisp shirt, skirt, or pair of trousers was a conscious meditation for her. I would sit at the kitchen table, where she did her ironing, and we would explore the questions I had about life and language and nature. She always answered me in a thoughtful way and offered suggestions based on her experience. While I sometimes found it difficult to apply these ideas to the daily challenges of childhood, I began to understand that a gap exists between what we internally know and what we can realistically express outwardly in everyday life.

Still, I remembered all of our discussions. Throughout my life they have empowered me, even when the train of my life felt like it was about to derail.

Even as a young child, I thought a little differently than my friends and schoolmates. I found I was always playing with words and painting colorful images with them. One day, I overheard my teacher say I had natural "Iambic pentameter" and, as only a child can reason, I thought this meant I had a disease! Worried as I was, I found I couldn't stop the constant playful flow of words in my head. Finally, I succumbed to my "illness" and wrote them down (I later learned this is called poetry). The acceptance of something that made me different allowed me to get back on the main track of my journey. It also prepared me for what was to come in expressing my inner voice.

My mother's philosophical leanings were balanced with my father's love of numbers and the reliable system they create when properly used. Dad was a 24/7 banker—he even did the books for our church. He showed me how to add things up and how different things related to each other and created a numeric balance. We also explored nature where he showed me how things grow, like in our abundant vegetable garden. One of the things he stressed was where to plant the "little ones" because 100% of what he planted grew into seedlings. Understanding numbers and nature and how to grow things became part of my main track too.

"Attitude is a little thing that makes a big difference." ~ *Winston Churchill*

Whenever I look out from the "caboose" and reflect on my journey so far, I realize how my various side journeys have resulted in fostering my lifelong passion for numbers, being positive, being curious about what combinations are possible, what works and what needs more pondering. By looking deeper, below the surface of events, I learned to tap into the inspiration available in them for greater happiness and joy. THAT is the personal call within for me—to look on the bright side and use it as a way to stay open to life's experiences. Hindsight has shown me that "answering the call from within myself" is about feeling good, taking inspired action, and living larger than I might have imagined through creativity while remaining grounded in my personal foundation.

Flash forward a couple of decades, from my dad's garden to my own happy marriage and motherhood, when I found myself being lured on yet another side trip. It showed up as a result of a powerful intention to express my voice—literally—as a host on Voice-America Internet Radio. As with many of my other adventures, I had no idea what I would encounter or discover along the way. But as author David Allen said, "The beginning is half of every action," and, so, I jumped in to host my own show.

The show, called "Mighty Gems – Spotlighting Everyday Jewels in Life," has served as a vehicle for me to share my personal discoveries and brought a whole new meaning to self-discovery. Why? Because making the choice to follow this calling meant that I could not just watch the scenery pass by outside my life train; instead, I learned that I was the artist responsible for painting the moving scenes of my life. It has been—and continues to be—a fabulous open-air experience that requires me to be present and active in each moment of now. The benefits of this are not always visible; however, that makes them no less profound.

As I get in touch with the essence of myself, my experiences, and my perceptions internally, the external moving scenery outside my train transform, and my life upgrades to match the most robust expression of my potential. This "side" journey of hosting a radio show is profound in that it is all about discovering the correlation between the words I use and the vibration they create in my life. As I change my words, upgrade my thinking, and improve my external communication, it directly affects the rhythm of my train. My world vibrates with a different frequency. Even more, I find I can create different results.

Universal principles teach that the frequency we operate from attracts more of the same to us, regardless whether we deem that to be "good" or "bad." Accordingly, I have learned that I can identify my operational frequency easier, and see how I am attracting new things into my life, by having clarity in my inner voice, then reflecting it externally in a bold way, claiming my words to describe exactly what I want to feel good.

The notion of having clarity is deceptively simple, however. It requires me to be awake and actively set aside time each day to practice the positive voice within myself. As the artist, I describe the scenes that I live every day. In speaking out loud the verbal articulation of what I want, I magnetically draw those experiences to me. It seems like a miracle but, really, it is pure manifestation through cause and effect.

The deeper discovery from this particular side trip is the importance of keeping my life adventure scenes clearly in view so I don't bring along "hindsight" baggage or waste energy looking for future scenes that are not mine. By planting the seeds of "letting go" and "being in the flow", I have learned that we explicitly create the pictures of what we want to bring into our life experience. For me, this is a Mighty Gem—an ordinary piece of natural material that becomes crystal clear and precious—that, with focus and a few key "mining" techniques, the picture I create inside will become my outer reality.

One caveat: you need to know that, if you choose this type of life creation strategy, you need to be fully conscious of all that is around you in your immediate world. It is important to be grateful for what you have created so far to empower yourself to create new results. What's "out there" is a reflection of what's "in here"—and vice-versa. Your surroundings are full of clues about the set point of your frequency, your daily self-talk, and how you interpret the world. Your environment is the result—the scenic imagery—you created yesterday (or last week or month or year). With that in mind, make sure you consciously choose your personal style and your traveling companions while you keep your desired journey at the forefront of your mental focus.

At times I've felt like I was pushing forward yet missing the connection to the scenery that was showing up. That was my cue to slow the momentum and focus more on the present scenery and opportunities that were showing up.

Now, by being awake and embracing what is happening in the moments of Now each day, I have calibrated my personal time zone (which I call Muse Time). Part of Muse Time is learning to embrace what it means to have Grace—ideally, on a regular basis. I have begun asking myself questions like "How can I simplify my choice?" or "How can I fully embrace and live in feel-good space all day?"

One opportunity that appeared to support me in feeling good all day was to learn how to practice Reiki. Interestingly, conventional methods of teaching Reiki include attending a weekend learning event that moves through the intellectual aspects of the modality. Given where my focus is—on aligning my inner and outer worlds with deliberate intention—I had to request a different way to learn Reiki. It needed to be on my time as opposed to someone else's fast train. I found my voice and created my reality on multiple levels.

So how does "Grace" factor into my story? When I look back to see all the seeds, side trips, and inspirations that have led me to where I am today, I am grateful for every moment. Each has been filled with blessings, some clearly so and some disguised as challenges—financial struggles, personal struggles, health issues like diabetes and cancer, various family issues and the loss of loved ones. Regardless of its outward appearance, each has been an opportunity for growth. My newest seedling is about listening to— and answering—the call within through the insight of NOW. And I'm grateful for it all.

Grace is present in every situation and I know I can access it at any time. All I need to do is pay attention, feel my train rhythm, and look out at my scenery.

ABOUT THE AUTHOR: D Lee is an author, talk show host, and businesswoman passionate about infusing her life with positivity and helping others do the same. From a very early age, she spent time in her father's garden, where she was first introduced to her internal Muse. Soaking up the positive beats of this busy environment, she learned the importance of systems and to explore present moments with all of her senses, embrace inspiring possibilities, and take empowered action with an "I can do this" choice. This perspective has given her greater resilience, creativity, and joy in her life.

D Lee – Mighty Muse, LLC
dmuse@themightymuser.com, themightymuser.com
essenceofauthenticpresence.com, mightygems.com
facebook.com/pages/The-Mighty-user/1435992000048864
twitter.com/MightyMuser

Beyond Hope
Darnell Florane Gouzy

It was 1992, and my life was going great; after years of operating a home-based nail business, I was finally preparing to open my own salon in a commercial area. It seemed as though all my plans were unfolding before me. But all of that was changed in one terrifying moment. The effects of those split seconds would last a lifetime, forever changing my life in ways I could have never imagined.

While waiting at a stop light, I heard a terrible sound, the kind of sound you hope you never hear behind you. Instinctively, I looked into the rear view mirror, tightening every muscle within my body. The kinetic energy of impact hit the trailer hitch first and shot the velocity through the main frame of the car. Gripping the steering wheel, I felt strange sensations shoot within my neck, shoulder, and back.

This was no ordinary auto accident; we were involved in a multi-car collision caused by a six-wheeled, two-ton truck going in excess of fifty miles an hour. My mind was screaming, "I have to be safe! My car has to be safe!" My six-year-old son was also in the car!

Thank God he was not severely injured. However, my injuries were quite extensive. After the accident, I could no longer extend my dominant arm away from my body without a partial dislocation of the shoulder occurring. I had sustained damage to the nerves and muscles controlling scapula and shoulder function. Ligaments from the base of my skull had partially torn away, making my head feel heavy and difficult to hold up for long periods of time.

Before the accident, I had felt empowered; I felt productive, as though I could conquer my small world and make it everything I had dreamed of. With imminent plans to open my business, I didn't have time to be injured! People were counting on me—my children, my husband, my parents.

After the accident, my life became so consumed by my injuries that they were controlling me, limiting me, and binding me with feelings of hopelessness, depression, and pain. How could this have happened to me? My life was planned and it was great! I didn't do anything wrong. How could I have fallen victim to this circumstance?

In those post-accident years, I was treated by thirteen doctors, all of whom were unable to significantly help me. My problems were caused by nerve and muscle damage, which caused scapula thoracic dysfunction and fibromyalgia, among other symptoms. One doctor suggested an experimental surgery to stabilize my shoulder by wiring my scapula to the back of my ribs! I decided against it because of numerous potential complications. Another doctor fitted me with a custom prosthetic device which consisted of a molded plastic shoulder cuff, sleeve, and scapula stabilizer that continued around by back and under my breast, eventually connecting to a strap to secure the device. This uncomfortable solution was less than optimal!!

In an attempt to deal with the torn ligaments in my neck, I began seeing a muscle disease and disability doctor who began a series of ten prolo injections. This procedure was also experimental, an attempt to re-injure the ligaments in a controlled setting, with hopes of reattaching them at the base of the skull.

Shuttling from doctor to doctor and from experimental treatment to experimental treatment, I felt trapped in a hopeless place with no one having a solid plan for how to set me free. I needed to get back to my life, but only fell into depression with constant pain and dysfunction. I remember one time when I was riding in a car that the pain was so intense that tears were running down my face. I repeatedly banged my knee into the car door thinking, *If I put my head through the window, the pain will stop!* And this was while taking multiple prescriptions and wearing a tens unit to control the pain.

Initially, I had an entire support system of people to help me through my recovery process. But as time moves on, so does life. People have lives, and my people needed to get back to theirs. The years were passing, and daily life continued to be a struggle for me.

I thought this was the end of my personal dreams and aspirations, the end of being a happy, playful mom who was able to be there for my children at the times when they needed me the most.

Through those years, I learned the truer and deeper meaning of patience and long suffering. I know now that it was the grace of God that sustained me beyond what I thought was possible. It was through this injury, this nightmare, that I came to know that I could either allow myself to fall into a place that I feared I would never recover from mentally, or fight through all that I believed to be true about my injuries and pain. Instinctively, I knew I had to distract my mind from the unhealthy part of myself and quiet the focus on my limitations as much as possible. I decided to join a choir, the intercessory prayer group, and later, the altar ministry at my church.

During an intercessory prayer gathering I was intuitively guided to place my hands into the container of prayer requests and begin to stir them around. I began to experience some type of expansion…of what seemed to be an expanded consciousness, a divine experience. I was in a vision and watched a river of water flowing from above. There were boulders blocking different areas within it and I witnessed myself laying hands on, and praying for each of them. Suddenly, my awareness was pulled back toward the room I was in. There was an intense wailing coming from inside and I wondered who else was there with me and what were they crying about? Then I realized, the wailing was coming from me!

As I watched what seemed to be a movie, I noticed that as each boulder moved to the side of the bank the intense wailing would quiet and the water would begin to flow! I was unaware a senior pastor of our church was present, but suddenly I heard him say, "Lord, move the boulders in the stream." This sent chills down my spine, because I realized he was seeing exactly what I was experiencing! I knew this wailing was for the collective cries of many representing every tear, problem and pain. It was then that I knew I was being called into the presence of true intersession.

As I focused on the needs of others, my own needs, pain, depression, and sorrow became less important. The screams within myself muffled, somehow, and I noticed that as I gave them less attention, they began to have less of a stronghold on me. I continued to experience a deeper sense of compassion and love for people—realizing that we can establish a connection with the Divine that allows an inner connectedness, a oneness, which had brought me to a level of empathy toward others that I never knew humanly existed. It was then that I realized the injury I thought would destroy me actually created an opportunity for the greatest personal growth of my life.

I decided to let go of all bitterness, anger, and frustration, and the feelings of "why me!?" My limitations and pain were still there, but I realized my life was being transformed. I was being used in a way I could have never been before the injury, and I am so grateful for those "lost" and difficult years.

Through the years, I continued to experience various levels of pain and dysfunction, but at a more manageable level with therapy and medication. I decided to seek treatment within the realm of complementary and alternative medicine. I turned to bio-field holistic therapies, seeking more relief. After a couple of sessions, I experienced a dramatic decrease in the pain and noticed I was able to use my arm in a way that made it more stable.

My positive experience with bio-field therapy made me want to help others in the same way. The experience fueled my desire to achieve certifications in Reiki and Pranic Healing. I began using these skills, as well as my church experience in intercessory prayer, and intuitively guided laying on of hands to help assist others in their recoveries—emotionally, physically, and spiritually.

When I began treating clients, a woman who had been experiencing a sense of detachment from life came in for a few sessions. I began performing standard techniques and noticed I was being intuitively guided throughout the session, knowing I was assisting in the removal of unhealthy deep emotional attachments. When the session was over she sat up and told me she'd had a profound vision. She saw herself standing at the side of a river bank, vomiting out emotional hurts and fears that had been holding her back throughout her life.

This amazing experience had reaffirmed what I already knew: that I was being called to do this work. The level of peace and divine connection a client experiences is priceless. My clients have expressed such deep, heartfelt gratitude for the presence of grace and peace during their sessions.

One told me that before the session she had been in a dark unhappy place. As I worked on her and for a long time afterward, she felt a sense of calm and tranquility. By the second visit she felt as though years of emotional scarring, baggage and pollution had been removed. The best way to describe it, she said, was a deep spiritual massage.

Another client had suffered from debilitating depression and anxiety for over fifteen years. She did everything, even lived in many places that were highly regarded for healing, such as the Esalen Institute in California, and although she had found some relief, it was never enough. I was so moved when she told me that she had never met anyone who did energy work in a way that was so grounding, demystified and intelligent. What she appreciated most was that I not only gave her the tools she needed to help herself, but to understand them. Thanks to God and the loving energy flowing through me, she was feeling better than she had dreamed she could and finally had hope for the future.

The simplest but most profound feedback I receive from clients is that my work helps them re-establish their relationship with the Divine. Some start praying or meditating every day, some just feel more grounded in their bodies and more connected to those around them. Thanks to my own experiences I knew this feeling well.

These comments and expressions of gratitude confirm to me each day that I am exactly where I should be in my life. I am forever grateful to God that through my personal experience of injury and pain, I became who I am today. Through grace, my brokenness became a healing of mind, body, and spirit. It is because of this experience that I am able to be used in a way I would have never known before, connecting with people in a deeper, more intimate way.

No matter what you're going through, or what you've been through, keep the faith. It is never hopeless. No matter how many years have passed while you have been waiting for your miracle, don't despair. Realize that in our worst and darkest days, a transformation may be in progress. It may simply be beyond what you can see or understand. Be grateful in all things so that the spirit of grace may sustain you until your time comes.

ABOUT THE AUTHOR: Bio-field practitioner Darnell Gouzy began her journey more than twenty years ago during intuitive "laying on of hands" at her church. After years of dealing with her own physical limitations, depression, chronic pain and fibromyalgia she sought treatment from a Reiki Master who worked within the energy body to bring her the relief she desperately needed. Her experiences led her to study energy-based holistic healing. Today, through God's grace, two Reiki Master Practitioner/Teacher certifications and training with the U.S. Pranic Healing Center/American Institute of Asian Studies, Darnell assists other with physical/emotional trauma and the stress of daily life. Darnell is also a member of the International Association of Reiki Professionals.

Darnell Florane Gouzy, RMT
Life Energy Therapies, LLC
lifeenergytherapies.net
lifeenergytherapies@gmail.com
facebook.com/LifeEnergyTherapies

Never Having to Know
Surabhi Kalsi

It was a regular kind of day, an ordinary day and I was running late (I visited a small temple near my house, every day; it was a spiritual practice I looked forward to). Halfway to the temple I realized I had forgotten to bring the scarf I used to sit on and pray, but I shrugged it off, thinking I would just sit on the floor.

As I entered the tiny enclosure, I saw a mat already spread out as if waiting for me. In all the days that I had been going to the temple, I never saw a mat lying around; the temple was usually empty. With a grateful heart I sat down on the mat and prayed. Just as I was getting up, I noticed the tattered edges of the mat. As I looked closely, it was a fabric ribbon and it had something written on it, repeating over and over. As I bent down for a closer look I realized with a start —it was *my* name written on that ribbon—over and over again —just the way I spelled it. I was truly taken aback. My name is not a common name, I never ran into someone in that temple on all my previous visits and here was a mat spread out for me with my name written on it. To me this was the biggest moment of Grace. In that moment, I realized that what is meant for me has my name written on it. It gave me an entirely different perspective to life.

Until then, I had lived from a space of "how things should be." It was a design cast in gold—the gilded life. I was always in fear of missing out on something. I wanted my life to be perfect and ideal just as this blueprint. I was on a deadline—to accomplish, to fall in love, to get married, to have children—it all had to happen according to the gilded plan. But as I sat in that tiny little temple on a tattered old mat with my name written on it—it finally hit me— yes, there is a plan for each one of us, a plan that is unique to each one of us. And everything, every experience will come to me— when the time is right for me. My world was my own unique expression of me and not a race against time to aspire to the ideal life. My life was ideal for me. There was a Divine plan unfolding for me. When I lived from this space there is nothing wrong, nothing missing, there is nothing to prove, there is no competition because everyone is a unique story unfolding with divine timing and perfect synchronicity.

As I sat there on that mat I also realized that I had spent a lot of time either worried about the future or thinking of the past. I was never present, *to the present*. How could I fill my life with worry when the Divine, the Spirit, the Universe took care of me in such a way, thinking of the smallest things? I was here asking God for something, something that I felt I didn't have, something that should have happened by now—and I was not present to the many blessings and the things that I do have in my life and did I say thank you enough? It was almost always about what wasn't there. And that is such a space of lack to be in. I was overlooking the abundant blessings of my life and choosing to focus on the lack, which came from the gilded plan of how life should be.

I looked back at my life, at all those times when I was running behind something or someone, trying to make things happen, trying to fulfill all the "should" of our society, all the expectations and the self-imposed deadlines of "this is how life should unfold"—so many times blaming myself or having the sense of not doing enough perhaps—that downward spiral of despair that pulls you down in a whirlpool of negativity. It all seemed so meaningless and futile, like trying to clench sand in my hands. I was living from a space of lack. For how could I lose what was meant for me? And what could I create from this space? More lack.

The mat opened my eyes to the many blessings I had in my life. I started to understand the meaning of Grace. The meaning of being present to All There Is. God or the Divine is *for me*, He is on my side. Nor am I alone. Nor am I disempowered, for He holds my hand at all times. When I look closely, I see the hand of God in everything. From this space, everything is a miracle. Everything is possible. I am grateful for everything including the unanswered prayers and all that is over for it was not meant for me. I started a simple practice of being thankful—writing down all the things I was thankful for at the end of the day, before I went off to sleep. As I wrote it down, I became present to it all. I felt Grace, I savoured it. And I anchored it in my life.

As I walked back home from the temple, I couldn't help smiling as I thought back to all those times I felt God didn't listen, when in reality it was I who had turned a deaf ear. God is listening and responding to us each and every moment. As I started being present I was free from the conflict, the worry, the anxiety of the past or the future, I started seeing the signs of Grace in my life more and more clearly. I was listening and the Universe was talking to me. It is a space of constant communion with the Divine.

The path of Grace and gratitude showed me many miracles. I consciously reached out to the Divine, to the higher powers, and one incident stands out—my pet dog Cookie had just passed away unexpectedly. His death came as a shock and I couldn't come to terms with it. I kept asking God and the angels to show me a sign, that he was okay. One evening, while out for a regular walk, I found myself suddenly guided to take pictures. No matter that it was dark and there was nothing to photograph, I just used the flash and clicked away. When I got back home, I went through them, and that's when I got my sign. There, in a series of pictures taken at the same place, I can see Cookie's face amongst the branches of a tree! It gets clearer with each picture and in the last picture I can see him clearly. I knew he was okay and I could let him go.

My work as an angel teacher made me witness so many things that brought me down to my knees. I once pointed my phone camera at the vast dark sky and said, Archangel Haniel, please come in my picture. As I clicked the picture, in the flash of light, I saw a perfect moon-shaped orb appear in the sky as a response to my request! And I captured it in my picture.

I was in Glastonbury recently and just before leaving I went to the Chalice Well to offer gratitude and to say goodbye. I always leave an offering here or tie a ribbon as a sign of my gratitude. As I was walking out, I had this insistent feeling that guided me to go to the Chalice Well shop. I tried to reason with it—I had visited the shop earlier and was all done with my shopping! My bags were all packed and I was ready to leave in a couple of hours. But knowing fully well the ways of the angels, I did go to the store. As I looked around, mentally asking the angels, *Why am I here?*, I noticed this beautiful, huge angel on one of the shelves, and I was guided to buy it! I tried to reason again—this angel is too big to fit in my luggage, I have no space in my luggage, I don't have much cash left and I have forgotten my credit card PIN! So how am I supposed to have this angel? I was browsing through the different card decks on display as I had this conversation with the angels. I randomly opened a box of oracle cards and a card fell out—it had a huge beautiful angel with its wings spread out, over the lion head at the Chalice Well. And the card said—the angel of the Chalice Well! Now I had no choice but to ask the store manager about the angel. I went up to her and inquired about the weight of the angel. "It's not heavy at all," she replied, "and I have a packed piece all ready to go in its original packaging!" I explained to her that I had forgotten the PIN of my card and she readily agreed to accept the card with my signature. And the angel came home with me.

The path of Grace is about trust and faith. It's about following the signs, following your guidance and instinct and knowing that life is unfolding according to Divine perfection. It's about honoring my journey, honoring myself and knowing that I am powerful Divine expression.

A major part of my life was spent fretting over or worrying about the future, the outcome, the destination. I lived in a sense of anticipation—what will happen? How will my life turn out? Will I be able to achieve my goals, follow the socially acceptable pre-decided path of how my life "should" unfold? Now I live from a space of never having to know. I live from a space of trust and surrender, for I see the hand of God in everything and I am grateful that I am present to it All.

Never having to know

As I walk You walk with me
Never having to know what enfolds
I know enough, today ~ for today
And I am happy to let tomorrow unfold

Never having to know who I will be
Never having to know the maybes
For I am happy to know
Never having to know more than this moment ~ now

Never having to know is sweet surrender
Never having to know is trust and wonder
Never having to know is the leap of faith
I know that and that is enough.

Never having to know is a state of Grace
Never having to know is the Kingdom of heaven
Never having to know is the whisper of angels
Never having to know, I can take it all for granted

Never having to know is your Grace and my miracle.

ABOUT THE AUTHOR: Surabhi Kalsi is a Heal Your Life® Coach, workshop facilitator, Angel teacher and Transform Your Life teacher with the Diana Cooper Foundation, UK. With a focus on creating balance between Mind, Body, Spirit and Heart, Surabhi combines spiritual, scientific and metaphysical principles to bring positive life change for her clients. Having travelled and lived across many cultures, she feels blessed to work with a wide spectrum of people. Surabhi is also a fashion designer and entrepreneur and holds degrees in fashion, IT and business management. She is the founder of Angeliccan—a line of conscious products created using the principles of crystal, aroma and angelic therapies.

Surabhi Kalsi
The Wellness View
surabhi-kalsi.com
surabhi.kalsi@gmail.com
twitter.com/SurabhiKalsi

Eat Wild:
Appreciating Nature's Bounty
Kathy Sipple

"Devote a day to food – Appreciate the mysterious intelligence that created food for your health and pleasure, and say a prayer with every connection to it..." ~ Dr. Wayne Dyer, *Change Your Thoughts - Change Your Life*

I follow our guide through the woods on this steamy summer day in Northwest Indiana, not far from Lake Michigan. I listen intently as she describes the importance of many plants along the trail. Her face brightens as she exclaims, "Blueberries! These are a sign of good conservation methods. If there were too many invasive species growing here, the blueberries would be choked out and could not grow in the middle of the woods."

She explains that hundreds of years ago, before European settlers arrived, insects, storms, and fire—set both by Nature and Native Americans—kept the conditions favorable for food growth. Waving her hand at the dappled sunlit forest floor, our guide says, "The Native Americans couldn't run out to the grocery store to pick up some food. This was their grocery store."

Her face darkens as she notices a plant. "This is garlic mustard. Early pioneers brought it over from Europe, likely for food and medicine." We learn that despite being high in Vitamin A and C, ecologists despise garlic mustard due to its invasive habit. Each plant has approximately 8000 seeds so it multiplies rapidly, crowding out many native plants important to the ecosystem's health.

The group continues down the hiking trail, but I hang back to try some garlic mustard. It tastes a little bitter, but mostly garlicky, not bad. I decide I'd like to learn how to "eat it to beat it" and immediately begin to wonder how much pesto I could possibly make in my effort to eradicate it. Next I pluck a tiny blueberry and savor its tart sweetness. I have a newfound interest in both of these food plants, each important in their own way to feeding long-ago inhabitants. These days, most of us just walk right by.

Off to See the Wizard

A few years later I sign up for the Indiana Master Naturalist Program. I'm interested in learning about all the natural resources in my state, but am especially excited about a workshop on wild edibles. The speaker reminds me of Gandalf from Lord of the Rings, with a long white beard and a huge, rough-hewn walking staff.

He shares with us decades-old slides of various dishes he prepared when he was a younger man and chef at a bistro specializing in wild edibles. The gorgeous images rival those in Bon Appétit Magazine, each dish more tantalizing than the next: stinging nettle soup, spring rolls with black locust blossoms, grilled ramps, and wild asparagus with sautéed morel mushrooms, wild plum tart...

He then provides us with a master list of the hundreds of wild edibles that grow in our area. Some—various berries and other fruits—are familiar and already known to me as edible; others I knew by name but had no idea I could eat them: cattails, day lilies (the flower, shoots, and tubers are all edible). Still others—purslane, lambs quarters, and chicory—I knew by sight, but knew neither their name nor whether they were safe to eat. The rest, I could never remember seeing before; those were the ones I set out in search of: black locust blossoms, paw paws, Japanese knotweed, ramps, morel mushrooms...

I remember the wizard's guidance as I try new dishes. As he advised, I start slowly with plants I can easily and confidently identify. I also learn whether they have poisonous lookalikes: moonseed looks like wild grapes; poison hemlock looks similar to Queen Anne's lace...

"Live in each season as it passes; breathe the air, drink the drink,

taste the fruit, and resign yourself to the influence of the earth." ~
Henry David Thoreau, *Walden*

In the spring I go crazy with dandelions, abundant in my yard
since we don't spray. Though I've never been a fan of chemical
weed killers because of its impact on the earth, now I find myself
thinking, *why would I want to kill off free food?* I make braised
dandelion greens, "coffee" from ground roasted dandelion roots,
and dandelion flower fritters. Triumphantly, I post photos of my
dishes on Facebook, proud of my resourcefulness. One concerned
friend messages me privately, "Are things okay with you guys? I
figure things might be getting pretty bad over there if you're starting
to eat dandelions."

I continue my obsession, unfazed. I discover a huge patch of
ramps (wild leeks) and make enough compound ramp butter to
freeze and use all year, ramp/garlic mustard pesto, and potato salad
with ramps. I learn about sustainable harvesting methods to ensure
the ramps keep coming back. The garlic mustard I collect with
abandon, being careful not to strew any seeds to prevent them from
invading new areas.

In summer I find myself torn between wanting to spend time in
my community garden plot and wandering the woods filling my
basket with elderflowers, blackberries and—as the season winds
down—elderberries. Though I still enjoy my homegrown tomatoes,
I find myself more and more drawn to the food nature offers readily,
without so much planning and prodding on my part.

In the fall I jar chutney made from the beautiful large crabapples
I gather at a local park. I get a lot of funny looks and even a few
questions from one young girl.

"Can you do that?" she asks as she approaches me.

I answer her question with a question. "Why, because you think
crabapples are poisonous or because this is a park?"

"Well, both," the girl admits, confused.

I explain to her that though crabapple seeds contain trace
amounts of arsenic, so do a lot of other foods, including regular
apples. I remove the seeds, so there is no danger. As for her other
concern, I have spoken to the park staff and they assure me they are

delighted to have less messy fallen fruit on the ground.

Several times a year I participate in something called a food swap. Attendees bring items that are homemade, homegrown or foraged to exchange with one another. This time, my table boasts nearly all seasonal and preserved foraged finds. I carefully set out samples of black locust blossom syrup, apple butter from foraged apples, Tkemali sauce from foraged wild green plums and gumbo filé powder made from dried and ground foraged sassafras leaves. The other swappers eagerly try my offerings and are just as eager to learn about the items themselves. I go home with homemade goat cheese from a local farmer, a dozen farm fresh eggs, a loaf of fresh baked bread, and other more traditional items. I look at my haul and think, not a bad trade-off for a few walks in the woods!

Visions of Mushrooms Dance in My Head

In the spring, I am eager to step up my culinary game. The fruits and vegetables are great, but my goal is to prepare meals of more substance. For this, I think I'll need mushrooms but have some trepidation about using them, having heard the cautionary tales of people poisoning themselves. On the other hand, I have always loved mushrooms and suspect I will love wild mushrooms even more. Plus, I have never had a morel. I need to find my own. When I learn about classes offered by the Hoosier Mushroom Society to become certified in morels and other wild mushrooms, I immediately sign up.

I am a bit disappointed that the mushroom classes do not involve actually looking for mushrooms. Instead, about 80 of us sit in a large lecture hall and learn from books and a PowerPoint presentation on a large screen. I pass the class and am now the mushroom equivalent of a notary public. I can certify mushrooms I or others find, making them legally saleable to local restaurants or at farmer's markets. Armed with this knowledge and my certification, I do what I'd been longing to since the classes began - head out to the woods!

I soon learn that knowing about mushrooms and actually finding mushrooms are two very different things. My husband joins me on these outings and although we find we are better mushroom hunters together, that first spring we find just six or seven morels. We joke that we would be very skinny (or dead) if we had to live off the land.

In the fall we look for Laetiporus sulphureus, known as chicken of the woods mushroom because its texture and taste are remarkably similar to chicken. I have purchased it in the past from a mushroom expert and am dying to find one on my own. These are noted as a good species for beginners to try because they are bright orange (fairly easy to spot in the woods) and have no poisonous lookalikes. My heart leaps when I spy a flash of orange on an overturned tree. Darn! It is an orange bandana someone must have lost on a hike. Back on the trail I see another glimpse of orange, but this time it's orange spray paint used to mark a tree destined to be taken down.

I'm disappointed and tired of looking so decide to give up, for today anyway. I find a spot on a steep ravine in the woods and marvel at how this place was formed by glaciers that stopped here after forming Lake Michigan just north of where I am sitting. All of a sudden, I don't want or need anything from the land. A gentle rain begins to fall and I don't move. I am deeply grateful to live in such a magical place and am content to drink in its beauty through the gentle mist. I close my eyes, wanting to remember this feeling of deep gratitude.

Opening my eyes again, I notice a tree on the other side of the ravine. Oh my! It is the biggest chicken of the woods mushroom I have ever seen and it is gorgeous! I wonder if nature is rewarding me for saying grace? I hadn't said thank you to the earth lately as I had been so caught up in finding food that I really didn't need to survive. I felt my relationship with the land had been restored through this reconnection and perhaps my vision had changed.

As I clean, cut, and sauté twenty pounds of mushroom, I remain in a state of profound gratitude for this beautiful "bird." I also see very clearly why it got its name. The "feathers" look like the traced fingers around a hand children often draw to create a turkey at Thanksgiving. I decide this mushroom will be our very own Thanksgiving dinner, tonight. Why wait until a particular day to celebrate nature's harvest?

Maitake mushrooms are known in Japan as 'the dancing mushroom'. According to a Japanese legend, a group of Buddhist nuns and woodcutters met on a mountain trail, where they discovered a fruiting of maitake mushrooms emerging from the forest floor. Rejoicing at their discovery of this delicious mushroom, they danced to celebrate. ~ Paul Stamets

ABOUT THE AUTHOR: Kathy Sipple resides just outside of Chicago near the Indiana Dunes with her husband John and their black Labrador retriever, Bodhi. She is a frequent keynote speaker and trainer and host of several podcasts. She holds a B.A. in Economics from the University of Michigan and is a member of Mensa. She won a Golden Innovator Award from Barbara Marx Hubbard and Conscious Evolutionaries Chicagoland for her empowering and groundbreaking work in social media. Sipple works online with clients everywhere to provide social media strategy, training, and coaching. For consulting info visit mysocialmediacoach.com or try her affordable group coaching program free for 30 days at cothrive.org/free.

Kathy Sipple
kathy@cothrive.org
cothrive.org
mysocialmediacoach.com
219greenconnect.com

A Reason, A Season, A Lifetime
Kathy Fyler

*People come into your path
for a reason, a season or a lifetime.
When you know which one it is,
you will know what to do with that person.
It is said that love is blind, but friendship is clairvoyant.
Thank you for being a part of my life...
Whether you were a reason, a season, or a lifetime.
~ unknown author*

A Reason

Sometimes someone shows up in your life and it isn't until years later that you recognize the face of grace.

In my twenties, I was living a dual life. I was one person at work and another in private. The two were very separate.

I was working as an RN at large teaching hospital in Connecticut, not far from where I grew up. I did the work thing—made friends, went to parties, climbed the ladder. No one knew (or at least I didn't think they knew) about my "other" life. I didn't even share this with my best friend Julie. We were friends since the first day we met during our orientation. We went on vacations together. I was in her wedding. We basically talked every day and talked about pretty much everything... well, everything except the fact that I liked women.

I remember the pains I would go through to keep my private life secret. I didn't talk about some of my other friends or the social gatherings I went to. I certainly didn't mention going out to tea dances or white parties, and I was always careful to say " I" instead of " we" when I shared what I did on my days off.

Then in comes Wendy, an ICU nurse with tons of energy. She

was fun, quirky, and totally authentic. She enjoyed doing things like kayaking and mountain climbing. She even camped on the side of a mountain—a mountain covered with ice–in the wintertime! So she really wasn't afraid of much. She didn't care what anyone thought about her. And the interesting thing was… pretty much everyone liked her. It didn't seem to matter that much to anyone that her life partner was a woman.

Wendy, Julie, and I spent a lot of time together. We organized a trip to Maine for several women from our nursing unit to camp and go white water rafting. We all studied together for our critical care exams. We worked the night shift and then had breakfast at the local diner.

Almost everyone was comfortable with Wendy. This would have been the perfect opportunity for me to "come clean" at work. Wendy had paved the way.

Unfortunately, I was so immersed in my "story", my work persona, that I still wasn't comfortable "coming out." I admired Wendy's attitude and authenticity—and was even a bit jealous of it. As for Julie, I moved out of state and our lives drifted apart. I never took the opportunity to open up and tell her about me. To this day, I regret that I didn't have the courage or the faith in her to talk with her about it.

I no longer live a dual life like I did back then. My family and friends know about and respect my relationship and they're all happy that I am happy. I live my life with authenticity and I am thankful for the lesson that Wendy gave me. If only I had learned it sooner...

A Season

There are certain chunks of time in life that hold a purpose beyond our imagination.

After our business folded and we were trying to figure out what was next for our business life, we attended a networking meeting for women. The woman, Pam, who led and organized the event was energetic and charismatic—so much so, that both Sue and I were excited about the prospect of learning more about what she was doing. At the time, she was creating events, hosting monthly networking meetings, and publishing a local monthly newspaper.

We attended several more of her events and spoke with her at length. We loved her mission for her company—or at least what we thought was her mission—to encourage, educate, and empower women.

She was also interested in what we could bring to the table. Sue and I were seasoned entrepreneurs, having just been named to The Inc. 500 Fastest Growing Private Companies, and we had grown our company to $5 million dollars in sales. We were actually looking for a new venture and this seemed right up our alley.

Our partnership with Pam was formed (informally). Interestingly, there were partnership papers to sign but it always seemed like there were more pressing things to do and we never did sign on the dotted line.

Over several months, we helped grow the company and added two more networking chapters and another newspaper in a nearby county. Sue and I worked tirelessly and for little to no money. This was okay because we saw the potential in the business and we were really enjoying what we were doing. There were many long afternoon meetings or times that we worked well into the night hours. We seemed to work well together and had lots of fun, with many outbursts of laughing so hard we cried. We were invited to family parties, dined with Pam and her husband, and made big plans for expansion.

Then something shifted; it seemed to happen overnight but there were subtle signs along the way. What we thought we were creating was now something very different from what Pam wanted. She was now (or maybe always was) interested in focusing on a more Christian, bible-based model, where we thought we were building a spiritual, global, inclusive company.

We were devastated! This was not what we signed up for (or didn't sign up for, thank goodness!).

Unfortunately, it was not an amicable split. We all felt betrayed, hurt, and misunderstood and our relationship was beyond repair.

The good news is that Sue and I found that we loved what we were doing and the industry was wide open and ripe. We had made incredible friends, built solid relationships, and had met a large number of contacts. We put together our newly-designed business model and in this season Powerful You! Women's Network was born.

A Lifetime

We have this wild and wonderful life to observe, to learn, to grow.

During my lifetime, I have been blessed with many beautiful examples of Grace. The most profound is my father.

My dad is a living example of Grace. He loves life and has great respect for it. He is not content in sitting around and letting life go by—he works hard and plays hard. In fact, he is like the energizer bunny—every day he continues to move until he sits in his recliner (or pretty much any chair) and falls asleep.

He is selfless and generous. About twelve years ago, his neighbor Judy was sick and in need of a kidney transplant. My parents were really close friends with Judy and they often went out to dinner or had cocktails together. They knew her prognosis wasn't very good and living the rest of her life on dialysis wasn't easy or appealing in the least. After discussing it with my mom, he got tested, found he was a match, and donated one of his kidneys to her. They recently celebrated thirteen years since the donation. Donating his kidney was a *huge* gift, and there were many small gifts too.

From him I learned to be kind and treat everyone the same. He would talk to the busboy the same as he would the richest guy in town. He was always kind and friendly, often starting conversations or joking around with whoever was standing next to him, whether he knew them or not.

Now that he is retired and living in a gated community in Florida, he has become the neighborhood handyman. If you look in his utility room, he has keys to all the houses on his street. When the snowbirds leave after the winter season, he takes care of things for them, making sure hurricane shutters are secure, the lawn crew does a good job, and their houses are safe.

He also seems to be the neighborhood chauffeur, driving friends to and from doctors appointments, hospital visits, and the grocery store... If they need him, he's there for them.

All of this at eighty years old, and I'm guessing he'll be doing it as long as he's able to. I'm blessed to be his daughter and happy that some of his goodness has rubbed off on me.

I also learned a lot from my mom, but that story is for another book.

•••

Reflecting on my life, I am grateful to have experienced so many good people, happy coincidences, and loving exchanges. I am keenly aware that I too am someone else's reason, season, or lifetime, and each day I ask for guidance to be a positive one.

ABOUT THE AUTHOR: Kathy's earlier career includes being a Critical Care Nurse, Project Manager for a technology firm, and owner of a $5 million manufacturing company. In 2005, Kathy followed her calling to make "more of a contribution to what matters most in this world." Using her experience and passion for technology and people, she co-founded Powerful You! Women's Network and Powerful You! Publishing to fulfill her personal mission of assisting women in creating connections via the internet, live meetings, and the published word. Kathy is an Amazon #1 Bestselling Author who loves to travel the country connecting with and teaching women.

Kathy Fyler
Co-Founder of Powerful You! Inc.
powerfulyou.com
powerfulyoupublishing.com
info@powerfulyou.com

The Dimensions of Our Existence and the Journey Home
Kathleen Burkard

Since the beginning of time, life after death has been humanity's greatest mystery and arguably one if its favorite topics of discussion. The philosophical, spiritual and scientific communities each have their own thoughts on the meaning of life and the after-life. I, however, will refer to the after-life simply as "home," for in my heart I know that we are all but visitors who chose to put their soul into a body, and when it is time for our spirit to return home, our life presence will have completed the role it was meant to fulfill.

We are energetic beings, just as everything on this planet is energy-based. We use that energy to create, to think, to invent, to grow, and to stretch our knowing. Our life experiences are vast and varied. There are many, many layers to what we know and do. Life is like an onion. We keep peeling and peeling away the layers, but there are so many that we hardly make a dent as we continuously cycle from one dimension to another. Our soul continuously expands with the knowledge we acquire and incorporates those experiences into our life-long lessons and one, never-ending journey.

As a child, I was very connected to the "other side." I also found it difficult to grasp some of the teachings of religion. One of the things that confounded me most (and still does to this day) is why we are so disconnected from our true home. We act like the other side is some random place that we will hopefully go to when we pass over. It is like we have disconnected our hearts from our true home when we decided to take our earthly walk. In this same vein, we are taught to pray to God for help and guidance, then, when we hear God's answers, we are considered strange and often branded witches or heretics, not to be trusted. This, too, has never computed for me; it is simply not logical. If you reference the bible used by Christians (I do not have knowledge of other religious teachings as I grew up Catholic), it is full of everyday people that God used as messengers of His word.

As I grew into adulthood, those niggling thoughts needed answers, or at least a deeper understanding if concrete answers were not meant to be. Eventually I was called to use my senses (all six of them) to seek this understanding that went beyond birth, life, and death.

For many, transitioning from our bodies back into spirit form seems to be quite a formidable journey. Many fears centered around pain, loss of dignity, the unknown, worthiness, and so on play into this transition. Many fear their imperfect selves will not be welcomed by God. I can only add to this what my heart tells me with a deep rightness, and that is God knows the truth that lies within our own hearts. He loves us as His children and His creation. He expects our failures, for that is how our soul learns and grows. God is forgiveness and love, and we never have to fear Him.

I have been given a unique seat to the viewing of death and have participated in the journey of transitioning home. I have learned much from these experiences, and have grown greatly in compassion and non-judgment as each soul's personal adventure was shared with me.

My first such experience, which occurred around eleven years ago, took me quite by surprise. In fact, it scared me, too!

One day I was doing laundry when my dog, Max, who had been sleeping on the stairwell landing, started barking. I went to investigate and found Max looking skyward. I immediately knew it was a spirit and asked it to leave if it wasn't there in God's light and love. As I moved back to the laundry room, I felt the energy of this spirit along my back. I recognized his goodness and the need to communicate with me. He was a young boy, about four or five years old, with blond hair and beautiful blue eyes. His name was David, and he had recently been killed by his abusive father. David indicated that he felt safe in my home as he liked my dog's and my energy. I asked him to go to the light and be with God, but he was fearful of what awaited him on the other side. He had lived through so much pain in his short life and was understandably trepidatious about venturing forth. David stayed with Max and me for about a week. We talked and Max helped to heal him as only a dog can do. He finally felt comfortable to let the loving energy of God flow through him and chose to follow it home.

Not long after this experience, I was guided by my angels to take a trip back to my hometown near Buffalo, New York. There was a strong urgency that I could not resist, and I knew it had to do with my grandma. Once I was on the plane, I inquired as to what was going on and was told that my grandma needed me to help her pass over. I immediately filled with fear and asked them not to have her die in my arms. That was just too much of an overwhelming scenario for me to comprehend. I wasn't sure what to expect after I arrived and took off for the nursing home to visit her. She had dementia, and for about the first half-hour of my visit, she did not recognize me. Then, suddenly she looked at me and exclaimed, "Kathy, I've been waiting for you"! Grandma was afraid of the death process and whether she was worthy enough for God to bring her home. She was also afraid that when it was her time, she wouldn't be able to go as she could no longer walk. I assured her that she would be in a perfect state, and I expected her to dance a jig on the way over. Well, she thought that idea was so funny—she even promised me that she would! After a few days with much discussion and many assurances, it was time for me to leave and go back to Chicago. I asked her if she was okay with it all, and she assured me that she was good and would be ready when the time came. It was a tearful good-bye for both of us.

However, as it turned out her story did not end there, but four months later when I indeed helped her cross over. Again, this was a very new experience for me, but such a beautiful one. Late one evening, in a meditative state, I was with her as she was floundering in a pool of water and very afraid. In life, grandma was very fearful of water. I pulled her from the water, and I took her into my arms and rocked her like a baby and calmed her down. She had just spent many days prior to this fighting her death. I let her know it was all going to be okay, and she could release her soul and go home. My mom called me the next day to tell me of her passing.

Another time I was awoken from sleep by a friend's tearful call. Her father, who had been in the hospital, had just taken a turn for the worse. She was rushing there now to see him. I offered up a prayer and settled back into bed for a bit more sleep. Spirit, however, had other plans. Suddenly I found myself energetically next to his bedside with his hand in mine. I began to sing his soul home (if you knew me, you would know that I cannot sing and that was a big stretch for me) and he left after a few minutes. My friend called shortly after that to let me know that her dad had passed, and I relayed my story. She was so happy to know that her father had someone there with him at the very end.

My final story of transition occurred with another soul named Paul, who was already in spirit. A friend and I were called to assess a home energetically as there was some odd "goings-on." Pots and pans moving about, shower curtains sliding back and forth, bedding-shifting, et cetera. The home was up for sale, and the owner was afraid all of this energy would affect the sale. We evaluated the situation and realized that there was no negative energy; the spirit just needed to be heard. The owner, who had had similar experiences with this said she felt comfortable talking to this spirit and finding his story. We left the house feeling our work was done.

It wasn't until I stopped for gas that I realized that I had picked up an extra passenger! Paul knew I could hear him and needed time to talk. I gave permission for him to come to my home. I learned he had not crossed over because he didn't feel worthy and was afraid God wouldn't welcome him. Can I just say how amazing this soul's energy was?! He had been about eighty years old when he passed away and was a real old-fashioned gentleman. I explained that God expects us all to fail and learn from those failures. That is why we are living our life, to learn. Paul mulled this over for five or six days, then decided he was ready to leave. First, though, he had some advice for me, for being out of body had given him a whole new understanding. He wanted me to stand in my power and not diminish who I am to make others comfortable. I needed to face my own self-worth issues and trust in my own destiny and the gifts that

God has bestowed upon me as there is a reason that will become clearer as time passes. I enjoyed his company and appreciated his advice immensely; in fact, I still miss him to this day.

As I come to a close, I want to share this last important life lesson that highlights the many layers of our existence. I met Simon, my eagle friend, four years ago at a Native American Festival. We connected right away, but I wasn't surprised as the Eagle is one of my Native Power Animals. I was upset by the fact that he was chained down for all to gawk at. He had this response for me:

"Hello my sister of Eagles. You have soared with us many times. Though you are in human form, your energy melds with mine and vibrates as one.

Thank you for your care and worry of my life in captivity. Though I am chained down so people can see me, it is my path. I sometimes meet those of strong, natural energy who see and seek the truth in all things. Your energy has helped me to feel as if I again soar through the heavens. Together we shall fly as we seek an alternate universe that allows us to shed our bindings and soar freely. Whether our bindings are there for all to see or in our minds, all have chains that hold them down. We can create our freedom no matter the circumstances. It all lies within. No one can do anything to you that you do not allow. If someone hurts you physically, you can choose to heal your body and release the pain and suffering so it does not remain a part of you. Give forgiveness to all for sometimes they do not understand what they do. However, this is my path, and I "choose" to learn and grow from where I am.

All have a choice and sometimes their choice is not obvious. Pull in my energy and my "seeing" abilities when you need me. I tend to fly above and "see" what others do not. As an eagle, this is your gift. Fly high my sister and join us as you seek the TRUTH in all.

Thank you for "seeing" the true me! Simon, Your Eagle Friend."

We must all work on rising above situations and releasing our judgments. Life is not one-dimensional and carries many, many layers that unfold in perfect timing. Our journey is complex and individual. No two are alike. By embracing the differences in those around us, we can all learn from those differences, too.

I feel nothing but gratitude with being a part of this journey in a very intimate way that has taught me so much about this process of cycling to a new state of being. Every soul is precious, and every soul has a unique story. Live in Grace and hold Gratitude in your heart. Love is what matters most, after all!

ABOUT THE AUTHOR: Kathy Burkard is the founder and owner of Sacred Fire Energy, which provides energetic release for emotional, physical and spiritual health. Kathleen is a Shaman Practitioner and has studied under a Cherokee Medicine Man, Standing Bear, for the last eleven years. This study has included many hours of self-discovery and Cherokee healing techniques. Kathleen currently apprentices with Standing Bear in her own practice, enabling her to work hands-on alongside him to reach deeper levels of healing and understanding. Since January 2012, Kathleen has also been a Healing Touch Certified Practitioner, whereby the practitioner uses his/her hands in a heart-centered and intentional way.

Kathleen Burkard
Sacred Fire Energy
sacredfireenergy.com
kathyburkard@yahoo.com
630-292-9116

The Unexpected Gift of Heartbreak

Carmel D'Arienzo

I had already been asleep for awhile when the phone rang. *Who could be calling me at this hour?* I didn't recognize the number but picked it up anyway. It was him.

"Hi Carmel, it's me…" he paused, then I hear a woman's voice. "…and Mary."

What? Why is his ex-girlfriend there with him and why are they calling me?

I knew they still had some financial connection, and that he was staying in a room in her house while starting a new business in the very expensive Silicon Valley area. Still, something felt wrong. A few days earlier he had told me that he had to cancel our trip to Miami because he needed to "handle" some things with her. He said she was very jealous—not wanting to be with him, but not wanting him to be with anyone else either. He needed to resolve this situation and said he would reach out when he could. While heartbroken, I almost felt like he was protecting me. But this phone call? How could he put me in this situation?

"I know everything, Carmel," she said snidely, "I know about Miami."

These words stunned me out of my sleep stupor and I could feel anger rise in my throat. She was treating *me* like the "other woman."

With a parched mouth, I eked out the words, "Why shouldn't you know everything—there is nothing to hide."

"How would you feel, Carmel? You have been doing all this with my fiancé." she replied.

WHAT? I felt like I was starring in a Lifetime movie, but had not been given the script.

"Fiancé?" I exclaimed in disbelief, "But you aren't together!"

"No, we never broke up," she insisted.

I could feel the rage rise in my chest and turned it on him. "Is this true? Were you telling me lies?"

"Yes, there were lies. I guess I misled you both." He said he felt terrible, but offered little in the way of explanation. I wondered whether he had any idea that in one moment, he had completely shattered my reality.

My mind scanned back. I had never once doubted what he told me about us or the challenges he faced. He assured me that while long distance was not going to be easy, it was going to be worth it. He called me his "happy accident" and declared that I was a gift from the Universe, that he could tell me things he couldn't tell anyone else, that he loved me and that he could see living the next fifty years of his life with me. He came from the same personal development world as I did and was working in a position close to a top thought leader where trust was a prerequisite. If that man could trust him, I figured, so could I.

Needless to say, I didn't sleep that night. As I tossed and turned in bed, I imagined all the words of love, affection and empty promises being washed down the drain. I was hoping this was a nightmare that would be over when I woke up.

Betrayal and deception are like a serrated knife—the cut is not clean and the wound goes deep. On the way into the heart, the knife passes the scabs of the previous betrayals and rips them open. For me there had been three in the last ten years. Each one on its own was not insurmountable, but the re-wounding and accumulation of all the lies, cheating, double lives and disappointment was greater than the sum of its parts and felt unbearable.

The internal thoughts began. *What a loser you are. You just can't get it right. You are a failure. How could you have believed him? Why were you willing to settle for this kind of situation? You are unlovable. It must be you. You weren't enough. You always pick emotionally unavailable men. You will never have true love and happiness.*

I could also hear the external whispers: *Oh that Carmel is just*

unlucky in love. Maybe it is something wrong with her. I knew
something was off. I tried to tell her but she would not listen. Love
is blind. What do you care—it's not like you were married to him or
anything. Consider yourself lucky.

The weight of all these broken relationships piled up on top of
each other made me feel ashamed and like a failure. It was difficult
to get out of bed or feel excited about anything. I lost faith in the
integrity of people and the goodness of humanity. This
disappointment triggered the bigger failings of being in my early
fifties and never being married and never being a mother. Darkness
crept in.

This wasn't the way the summer was supposed to go. We had
worked through the challenge of the distance and had been
scheduled to celebrate our birthdays by going to a spiritual retreat in
Miami. All the angels aligned to make it happen. I had been hosting
a daily Gratitude webcast and began to experience the magic that
comes from focusing on what we appreciate. Even during the
challenging times, I would write down one thing about him and/or
the relationship that I could be grateful for in that moment and put it
in a Gratitude Jar. I was excited and feeling like the Universe was
conspiring in my/our favor. I had sublet my apartment in the city to
spend the summer out at the beach to concentrate on all the projects
I wanted to create for my work and the future. Now I felt like it had
been some big cosmic misunderstanding.

How could I have known that all these things I had set in motion
BEFORE that fated phone call, would actually be my saving grace
to move through the darkness?

Because I was committed to hosting the daily Gratitude webcast,
I had to get up that next morning and lead people on video.
Ironically, the topic for the day was Magical Relationships and I
invited my participants to think of three people they were grateful
for and why. My eyes were swollen and close friends could tell
something was up. Tears ran down my face as I led the group and
asked them to reflect on what they could be grateful for, even in
challenging relationships. I knew I had to listen to my own words.
Who was I becoming from this? I remembered the teaching *Life*
does not happen TO us, it happens FOR us. I was grateful that I

could look at myself in the mirror with a clear conscience. I was grateful that I was not grieving alone. I was grateful for the hidden lesson even if it was not completely apparent.

Each morning as I set up my tripod and hit the *Go Live* button, I was there for my participants, and they were there for me right back. I felt the collective human experience. Slowly, I could feel the smile come back as I felt the gratitude in our hearts strengthen each other.

Right after the webcast, I would ride my bike down to the beach. No one was there, save the seagulls. The only sounds were the lapping waves and the random chirping bird. It was here, in private, that I would shed my tears and then go in the water to wash them away. I would swim out as far as I could go and roll over onto my back. With my arms and legs stretched out, I floated, supported by the salt water that was keeping me buoyant. I looked up at the cloudless blue sky and over at the expansive landscape surrounding me. It was here I felt God/Universe/Sprit.

"Have mercy on me," I would, say, "Make haste to help me. Do your will in my life. I surrender."

And I let everything go. As the golden sun warmed my face, I knew this time it would be different. This time, the recovery would not be as long. I wasn't broken and I was not the same woman I'd been two years earlier. I had started so many great things in my life. I just made a mistake by lowering my standards with this man. I began to feel I could trust that there was a divine guide. How else would I have known to sublet my apartment? This is where I was meant to be to heal. I went deep into inquiry: What could I learn? What could I be responsible for? How can I see this as the gift it is and be truly grateful for it? I sent him a text, forgiving him in order to release him. Slowly, magic started happening.

Since he was no longer rooming with me in Miami for the meditation retreat, I had to find a roommate. I met Andrea and we became fast friends. The retreat was transformational as I learned the power of choosing to not indulge in suffering and not let one challenge, one disappointment become my identity. I learned that being in a state of gratitude is considered a beautiful state and the best place from which to navigate life. When one of the teachers from India hugged me on my birthday and said "I wish you peace, joy and love. Welcome home," I knew this was a turning point.

Whereas a few weeks earlier, I felt I had a right to suffer because this guy had completely deceived me and threw me under the bus, now I felt empowered to choose how I wanted to design this next chapter of my life. I started sleeping through the night, I ate and felt healthy and the smile on my face got a little bigger as I continued to focus on my blessings.

At one of my low points, my aunt saw me crying and asked, "Why don't you go to Italy?" I had lived there for some years, and she knew it was a place that brought me joy—where I felt alive and radiant. Unfortunately, a trip wasn't possible, but it made me think. Why do the female protagonists in books like *Under the Tuscan Sun* and *Eat Pray Love* go to Italy? What is it about Italy that helps them heal and why can't I experience that here?

The next morning, creative impulses woke me at 5:30 am. The words rushed to come out of my heart and onto paper. I created a five-day online program for people to feel like they are on holiday in Italy without ever leaving home. I don't know where the ideas where coming from—they just flowed through me. Over sixty people signed up. I let my imagination be their eyes to my world. I helped them—and myself—reconnect to passion, joy, love, presence, and family—Italian style. I played music to trigger our emotions and together we ate Nutella straight from the jar. I felt alive and on purpose again.

Had it not been for this man cracking my heart wide open, this buried treasure would never have been discovered. My new mission was so clear. As I helped myself, I could reach back and extend a hand to help other women transition from a painful ending to a new beginning.

While no longer at the beach, I still felt supported and kept afloat by a force greater than me. I was falling in love with my life again and teaching others to do the same. I was releasing to receive and was so grateful. People and opportunities, including this book, magically appeared in my life.

Although I sometimes looked back at the closed door, I made sure to linger only briefly, for the new one was swinging wide open and I did not want to miss my chance of walking through it. With grace and trust, I could now feel only gratitude for the experience. This man came into my life to teach me a lesson and then was pushed out of it so he would do no more harm. I learned how to set new standards and to set boundaries. I learned to value actions more than words. I recalled my motto— "Live Boldly. Love Deeply. Impact Greatly"—and realized I had done just that this summer. It didn't turn out as I had envisioned, but it was so much better. Steeped in trust, without having to control or needing to know exactly how, I stepped into a state of wonder and curiosity at what was coming next. And I was grateful for it all.

ABOUT THE AUTHOR: Carmel D'Arienzo is a certified transformational coach, speaker, and passionate lover of life. Her global ventures include opening Italy's first American bakery to organizing wine tours in Tuscany. From her years in Italy, she learned the secrets to living a "Bella Vita"—a beautiful life. Her mission, drawing on the best of her Italian and American experiences, is to help women in transition awaken their feminine power within, reconnect to their heart, and ignite new beginnings in their lives. Her daily gratitude practice webcast—Cappuccino with Carmel - The Gratitude Café has reached thousands. Carmel can best be described as "Under the Tuscan Sun" meets personal development.

Carmel D'Arienzo
Lifestyle Coach and Speaker
carmeldarienzo.com
carmel@carmeldarienzo.com

Always With Me

A Daughter's Journey of Grief and
Healing through Grace and Gratitude

Ana Conlin

It was a Saturday morning, 3:15 am to be precise, when I was startled from what appeared to be a two hour sleep, a loud ring sounding by my left ear. My eyes opened into a stare, and I held my breath. As my heart continued to accelerate I could feel the stillness of the night, and hear the sound of a bird by the window. The street light created a shadow through the bedroom window. I was at the Marriott Hotel in Aguadilla, Puerto Rico, which seemed to be turning into my new home. The phone rang again. Fear now setting in, I could feel the adrenaline rushing through my veins. Was this the call I'd been dreading?

Slowly picking up the phone, I heard a stranger's voice on the other end, and I realized it was the voice of a male nurse where my father was hospitalized. I said hello and braced myself for the unbearable.

...

As my plane descended into Aguadilla Airport, the fear of the unknown gave me chills. Something's not right. Everything around me felt like signs of something to come. Half an hour later, my sister and I walked into the hospital, our hearts breaking. The playful, funny and stubborn man who'd raised us was now laying still in his bed. It was heart-wrenching to see the expression on his face, with a delicate stare signaling his surrender to a feeding tube through his nose. Did he recognize us as his daughters? I hugged him gently, holding back my tears as I whispered in his ear, "It's me, Ivy." Hearing the childhood nickname, he had given me jogged his memory. He recognized me.

We were immediately confronted with a very grave and painful situation. What had started out as a small wound on his foot the year before was now a stage 3 and 4 wound with MRSA and gangrene. His only option was to have his leg amputated, with no guarantees of survival or quality of life. Otherwise, it was only a matter of time before sepsis set in and took his life.

While we didn't have a crystal ball, I did have my intuition, which had been honed over twenty years working in the healthcare space. I had also advocated for my grandfather three years prior. After consulting with my sister and our stepmom we decided to take a proactive approach; I was in charge of advocating on his behalf and collaborating with the clinical team coordinating his care plan.

Easier said than done. While one physician advised he had six months to live, the other advised his time was limited. With my medical background, this was a dilemma I knew all too well. This time it hit close to home; there was no time to be the grieving daughter, instead I chose to be my father's warrior, advocate, and protector.

We stood by, horrified, as the wound care nurse treated my father's foot. What was once healthy skin was now gangrene travelling up his leg. Thankfully, though, he was not in pain; not only was he on strong antibiotics and other medications, but the lack of circulation in his leg numbed all sensation. Still, my heart ached watching my father—my warrior—slowly deteriorate.

I still remember how painful it was for him when the orthopedic surgeon made one last attempt to schedule a full leg amputation. In response to the doctor's plea resilience set in, and he quipped sarcastically, "You will first cut my head before you cut my leg." He managed to turn a nightmare into a joke. I wiped my tears, happy to see him having a lucid moment, and smiled in admiration of his bravery.

Despite knowing the consequences of not having his leg amputated, we supported his decision. He would rather let the sepsis take him than go through a surgery that might leave him with no quality of life.

I understood, but I was furious, not with my father, but with God. How could He allow such a good man to suffer so much? I could not relate with my father's brothers and sisters encouraging me to pray for his healing. Could they not see he was dying? I could not leave it up to chance or faith alone, I had to do something and that meant fulfilling my father's wish to be buried in Puerto Rico, his birthplace and his father's final resting place. Finally, my sister and I made a final attempt to obtain approval so that construction could begin at our grandfather's burial site.

Anger turned to fear and desperation. This marked a sequence of events that would later restore my faith in a higher power, and bring on the realization that my family's efforts to keep hope at bay were not in vain. Every day I walked into the hospital, not knowing if this day would be his last. My fear of having to contest an intubation order was constantly on my mind. My dad had signed a healthcare proxy refusing intubation, and resuscitation a year prior. While at the dialysis center the social worker had a conversation about faith with him influencing him in his vulnerable state to sign papers he could not see due to his partial blindness from diabetes. We were confronted with a legal document that did not honor my father's original wishes. I knew I could contest the papers and win but what good would that do if a decision had to be made urgently? I was grateful that my stepmother would have the final say. I knew she would honor his wishes.

When my uncle told us he would approve burial at the family site, in a state of gratitude my sister and I headed straight to the cemetery. When the director heard the urgency of the situation, he agreed to help us.

Now my sister and I faced another quandary. We were scheduled to fly home the same week days apart, but were torn about leaving our father. The conflicting prognoses from the physicians were no help—one estimated he had six months; the other said his death was imminent. My sister made the agonizing decision to leave as planned, but would return in a few days. I chose to stay.

On Friday March 28, I checked in with the cemetery staff on my way to the hospital. Despite having other projects on his plate, the director and his crew had begun work immediately; what would have normally taken two weeks was almost completed in a few days. It was part of a Divine plan and he and his crew were our angels, much like my stepmother was in caring for our father unconditionally.

As I went to greet my father, our eyes met for the first time in what seemed like forever. Was he lucid? Did he know it was me? Yes, he followed my eyes and my movement until I approached him at his bedside.

"Are you tired?" he asked.

With that simple question, my heart filled with joy. All my life I had wanted to desperately be the daughter protected by her father. I knew he loved me, I just wanted to hear him ask me directly how I was doing. In that moment instead of the warrior, protector, and advocate I was the grieving daughter. I immediately smiled and hugged him, and told him not to worry—I was fine and I wasn't going to allow anything to happen to him either. I felt proud that my father trusted me with his life, that he believed that I would always overcome any situation.

I kissed him gently on the forehead, told him to get some rest. I was going to go back to the hotel to lie down myself so that I could stay with him from 4am until the next day. My stepmom's birthday was only a few hours away. She too needed the rest, but she insisted on staying. As I walked out of the hospital, I was once again consumed by the feeling that I may never see him alive again, and burst into tears.

...

The phone rang at 3:15 am. The male nurse instructed me to get the family together, the time was coming. I told him I was on my way, and called my sister in New Jersey. She picked up right away, as if expecting the call, and told me to drive safely. Later I would find out that minutes before, she'd had a dream of my father smiling and waving at her.

No matter how much I thought I could prepare for this moment, speeding down the empty highway, I realized that *nothing* could have prepared me. I began to bargain with God; I prayed to my lost grandfather, asking for the time to hold my father's hand as he transitioned into his new journey. I prayed for the strength to endure the unbearable. Yet at the same time, a part of me was also in denial. The conflicting chatter raged in my head, and before I knew it I was at the hospital. What would normally be a twenty-minute trip had taken me ten.

As I slowly exited the rental car and headed to the hospital entrance, my senses kicked into high gear. I could smell the tropical plants. The night was quiet and calm. Suddenly, something on my right caught my attention. It was a beautiful tree in front of the hospital. The brightness from the street lamp permeated some of the leaves. At that moment, what seemed to be forty birds flew from that tree to another in the parking lot. Simultaneously I felt like something around me lifted. I felt peace in that moment. The birds began to sing a beautiful melody that I never witnessed before and in that moment I knew my father was gone.

My heart aching with grief, I took a breath and headed inside. The security guard did not look me in the eyes but instead bowed his head, confirming my gut feeling, but still I clung to the hope that I could be there to hold my father's hands as he transitioned.

It was not to be. I reached the second floor nurses' station and found the nurse who had called me; the look in his eyes confirmed the unbearable. I let out a scream, then felt the nurse's arms go around me, catching me as I fell.

The long-dreaded moment had finally arrived. I slowly opened the door, then stopped short as I saw my father's lifeless body. Was this really happening? I took a deep breath, exhausted but grateful that he had gone peacefully. He was now on a new journey. I went back into the warrior and protector role. Somehow in that moment of pain and gratitude I was able to help cleanse his body, help cover him, and finally help my heartbroken stepmom find the strength to walk back into the room and touch him. As I watched her place her lips on his face, I knew I was watching an angel here on earth giving my father a farewell kiss. I felt a rush of gratitude for her; she had cared for my dad and I wanted to protect her as well.

We all came together to give my father the goodbye he so richly deserved. My husband went to get my dad a new suit, nothing but the best. In Puerto Rico the wake and funeral are very different than in the States. A wake is typically a twelve-hour day followed by four hours the next, somehow I found the strength to bear it. I was the first to see my father at the funeral home and spend some quiet time with him. We had a beautiful service, then my sister and I were allowed to sit in the front seat of the hearse transporting his sacred body. I felt like I was drowning when we drove by his home, but I took comfort in the fact that we had fulfilled his last wishes.

Just as the flocks of birds flew from one tree to the other on the morning of my father's passing, two birds began singing at his burial. In that moment of emptiness, I was reminded that I am not alone, he is always with me. It's not a coincidence that every time I visit his tombstone birds are always singing around me. Whether it is an anniversary or a visit to his grave, I am always accompanied by two doves flying above me. On the first anniversary of his death, two doves flew around my sister and I, letting us know he will always be with us. I put my trust in a higher power and know we are all part of a divine plan greater than ourselves. As Mitch Albom says, "Life has to end, but love doesn't." The fear of losing a loved one is a fear I know all too well and one that I will confront continuously throughout my life. But by putting my focus on a divine power and finding courage through gratitude I am slowly healing and learning to overcome the unbearable. I no longer fear death, I crave life.

ABOUT THE AUTHOR: Ana is the founder of Conlin Creative Resources, LLC and Ana Conlin Empowered, Professional, Innovative Coaching. She helps businesses and thought leaders co-create new direction, inspiring them to take bold action. Her mission in life is to lead and serve with passion, purpose, and integrity. She writes books designed for business and personal growth. Ana earned a B.A. in Psychology from Kean University. She holds numerous certifications such as Executive Leadership, Life and Master Business Coach, Assisted Living Administrator, and licensed practitioner of Neuro-Linguistic Programming. In addition, Ana is a Public Speaker, Business Strategist, and Author.

Ana Conlin Empowered Professional Innovative Coaching
Conlin Creative Resources, LLC
AnaConlin.com
Support@AnaConlin.com
facebook.com/CoachAnaConlin

About the Authors

**Are you inspired by the stories in this book?
Let the authors know.**

**See the contact information at the end of each chapter
and reach out to them.**

They'd love to hear from you!

Author Rights & Disclaimer

Each author in this book retains the copyright and all inherent rights to their individual chapter. Their stories are printed herein with each author's permission.

Each author is responsible for the individual opinions expressed through their words. Powerful You! Publishing bears no responsibility for the content of the stories by these authors.

Acknowledgements & Gratitude

WE ARE SO VERY GRATEFUL for all of the beautiful individuals and divine circumstances that united in grace to make this book a reality.

To our authors, we are humbled by and in awe of the openness, willingness, and determination you demonstrated in sharing your stories. Each of you is a gift to us and the world and we are happy to align ourselves with you. We are grateful to share in this next step of your purposeful journey of assisting and inspiring others. You are a blessing.

To our team—you know who you are–we thank you for your constant support, expertise, guidance, and love. They say it takes a village, and we are truly grateful that you're part of ours. We love you.

To our editor, Dana Micheli, we thank you for your professional and compassionate insights, your time and commitment, and the beautiful energy you share with our authors.

To our trainers Linda Albright, Kathy Sipple, and AmondaRose Igoe: We thank you for sharing your expertise, experience, and enthusiasm with our authors. By assisting them to get their message out into the world, you are helping more people than you can imagine. You're all rock stars!

To Jo Englesson, Creative Peacemaker and incredible woman who wrote our Foreword, thank you for your beautiful definition of gratitude and for teaching and being a living example of gratitude and grace in action.

To our friends and families, we love and honor you, and wish we could be "live and in person" with you more often. Our hearts are with you.

And lastly, we are grateful for our divine connection and the always plentiful supply of inspiration surrounding us each day. We are truly and abundantly grateful for this life. Namaste`

With much love and deep gratitude,
Sue Urda and Kathy Fyler

About Sue Urda and Kathy Fyler

Sue and Kathy have been friends for 27 years and business partners since 1994. They love their latest venture into publishing individually-authored books to provide a platform for individuals to achieve their dreams of becoming published authors.

Their pride and joy is Powerful You! Women's Network, which they claim is a gift from Spirit. They love their mission of gathering and connecting women for business, personal, and spiritual growth. Their greatest pleasure comes through collaborating with the many inspiring and extraordinary women who are their authors and a part of their network.

The strength of their partnership lies in their deep respect, love and understanding of one another as well as their complementary skills and knowledge. Kathy is a technology enthusiast and free-thinker. Sue is an author and speaker with a love of creative undertakings. They both know the immense power of feeling good and they love helping people do this in their lives. Their honor for and admiration of each other is boundless.

Together their energies combine to feed the flames of countless women who are seeking truth, empowerment, joy, peace, and connection with themselves, their own spirits, and other women.

Reach Sue and Kathy:
Powerful You! Inc.
239-280-0111
info@powerfulyou.com
PowerfulYou.com

Powerful You! Women's Network
Networking with a Heart

OUR MISSION is to empower women to find their inner wisdom, follow their passion, and live rich, authentic lives.

Powerful You! Women's Network is founded upon the belief that women are powerful creators, passionate and compassionate leaders, and the heart and backbone of our world's businesses, homes, and communities.

Our Network welcomes all women from all walks of life. We recognize that diversity in our relationships creates opportunities.

Powerful You! creates and facilitates venues for women who desire to develop connections that will assist in growing their businesses. We aid in the creation of lasting personal relationships and provide insights and tools for women who seek balance, grace and ease in all facets of life.

Powerful You! was founded in January 2005 to gather women for business, personal and spiritual growth. Our monthly chapter meetings provide a space for collaborative and inspired networking and "real" connections. We know that lasting relationships are built through open and meaningful conversation, so we've designed our meetings to include opportunities for discussions, masterminds, speakers, growth, and gratitude shares.

Follow us online:
Twitter: @powerfulyou
facebook.com/powerfulyou

Join or Start a Chapter for
Business, Personal & Spiritual Growth

powerfulyou.com